study daily

THE OLD TESTAMENT

ZACHARY COWAN

Copyright © 2018 Zachary Jeffrey Cowan

All rights reserved.

"This material is neither made, provided, approved, nor endorsed by Intellectual Reserve, Inc. or The Church of Jesus Christ of Latter-day Saints. Any content or opinions expressed, implied or included in or with the material are solely those of the owner and not those of Intellectual Reserve, Inc. or The Church of Jesus Christ of Latter-day Saints."

All published works cited by The Church of Jesus Christ of Latter-day Saints are used with permission © Intellectual Reserve, Inc.

All published works cited by Deseret Book are used with permission © Deseret Book Company.

ISBN: 1979208611
ISBN-13: 978-1979208611

ACKNOWLEDGMENTS

I have been born of amazing parents. Their example, faith, and service has always been a high-water mark. I am thankful to a God who sent me to them. I love my brothers and sister, who allowed me to live, and only remind me I am an idiot when I am really being one. I wish to express gratitude to the towns and people of Cedar City, my first home, and Salina, my current home. My love goes out to my leaders, teachers, and friends. They lit fires in me. I hope it is contagious. I won the heart of my wife, Katie, with a toe touch, a wink, and a smile. She captured mine when I realized that I didn't have to be a different person when I was with her. I love you, Lady. Boys, oh my beautiful boys—I love you for the demolition crew that you are and the men you will become. Thanks to Launa Albrecht for cover design. Brian Passey has been a professional for as long as I have known him. This book is worth studying because of his hard editing work. I wish to thank Heavenly Father, Jesus Christ, and the Holy Ghost. They have been abundantly kind to me. My eyes are not large enough to behold all their blessings.

Table of Contents

Introduction. 1

Books of the Pearl of Great Price

Moses. 2

Abraham. 16

Books of the Old Testament

Genesis. 11

Exodus. 37

Leviticus. 51

Numbers. 53

Deuteronomy. 63

Joshua. 67

Judges. 72

Ruth. 76

1 Samuel. 78

2 Samuel. 85

1 Kings. 88

2 Kings. 94

1-2 Chronicles. 101

Ezra. 101

Nehemiah. 103

Esther. 105

Job. 106

Psalms. 108

Proverbs. 110

Ecclesiastes. 112

The Songs of Solomon. 113

Isaiah. 114

Jeremiah. 138

Lamentations. 146

Ezekiel. 147

Daniel. 152

Hosea. 156

Joel. 156

Amos. 157

Obadiah. 158

Jonah. 159

Micah. 160

Nahum. 161

Habakkuk. 161

Zephaniah. 162

Haggai. 163

Zechariah. 163

Malachi. 166

Bibliography. 169

Introduction

Having recently been fired from their jobs, a baker and a butler found themselves not only on the unemployment list, but also cast into prison. God in His kindness gave an insightful dream to each of these men to prepare them for their unique future. Neither was able to understand this dream on his own, and it caused them to feel confused, alone, and scared. At this critical time, they encountered Joseph, a very capable guide, who was also in prison. When Joseph heard of the dreams he said, "Do not interpretations belong to God?" (Genesis 40:8). When Joseph asked that question, the dreams and the mercy of God were opened and both men could then properly prepare for their futures. When we ask good questions while reading the scriptures, it allows God — through the Holy Ghost — to give us interpretations and prepare us for our own unique futures. This book will ask the questions to help you receive insights and get direction and interpretations from God as you study the Old Testament.

How can this book be helpful to the youth and seminary students?

Youth are often taught to study the scriptures, but many have never been taught how to study, so instead they spend their time simply reading the scriptures. When they do this, they occasionally find a gem, but the context, and even the content, of this jewel is often misunderstood. Thus, most youth have a spiritual experience reading scriptures, but they do not receive all of the rich and powerful blessings associated with studying the scriptures.

In your Topical Guide look up "Scriptures, Study of." Don't worry about looking up any of these verses, just read through what is there and use the space below to make a list of words that describe how the scriptures should be studied.

_____

_____

_____

The very next entry in the Topical Guide is "Scriptures, Value of." As you read through these references, make a list of all the Lord's promises for studying the scriptures and not just reading them.

_____

_____

_____

Day 1, Introduction to the Bible and Old Testament

In the LDS Bible Dictionary, look up "Bible." As you read this entry, look for answers to the following questions:

If someone asked you what the Bible was, how would you explain it?

What is the significance of the word "Testament?"

What did you learn about the order, text, and language of the Old Testament?

What did you learn about the order, text, and language of the New Testament?

With so many new manuscripts and translations, why does The Church of Jesus Christ of Latter-day Saints still use the King James Version or the KJV?

How does Article of Faith 1:8 help us to have confidence in the Bible, even though there are several problems with the text?

Day 2, Moses 1:1-11

Because of the struggles mentioned yesterday about the text of the Bible, the Lord commanded the prophet Joseph Smith in 1830 to make an inspired translation. Many of these changes are not to restore truths or words that were lost, but to make adjustments so that the text is easier to read. The Book of Moses in the Pearl of Great Price is not a clarifying statement, but an example of a received revelation that provided additional information to the book of Genesis. Moses 1-8 is an inspired translation of Genesis 1-6:13.

The Book of Moses begins with a captivating vision that happens after Moses has fled Egypt and seen the burning bush. At this point in his life, Moses is unsure about who he is; he doesn't know if he's rich or poor, if he's a murderer, prince, fugitive, vagabond, or shepherd. The Lord is going to provide Moses with a correct orientation and purpose. In verses 1-11, search for what Moses learns about himself and what he learns about God. Why is what Moses learned so important for a person to know, especially those who don't know who they are? In what ways has this knowledge provided direction to you?

How many times did the Lord call Moses "my son?"

In verse 11, the term "transfigured" was used to describe the temporary change that happened to Moses so he could endure the presence of God. What can you learn about transfiguration from verses 1 and 9-11 in Moses 1 and from Doctrine and Covenants 67:10-14?

Day 3, Moses 1:12-23

When Moses is weakened and alone, Satan tempts and attacks him by belittling him and using fear. Which of these same tactics does Satan use on you?

In verses 12-23 look for what Moses learns about Satan and how he used what God taught to him in yesterday's verses to resist Satan's approaches.

It may seem like Satan is rather foolish to approach Moses and ask him to "worship" him (:12, 19). Moses responds that he will only worship God (:13, 15, 17, and 20). Satan doesn't approach us asking us to fall on our knees and bow before him, but he still seeks our worship. Worship is not merely shown by the recipient of our prayers, but is manifest in how we spend our thoughts, desires, time, and skills. Which of these do you use to worship God and which might compete with your worship?

In verses 20-21, what did Moses receive when he called upon the Lord for help? When was the last time you received the same thing when you called upon God for help?

Day 4, Moses 1:24-42

Following the attack from Satan, Moses again calls upon God (:24). Search verses 25-29 and discover what God told Moses about his calling, and what

God showed unto Moses.

After seeing this inspiring vision, Moses wants God to tell him why and how all these things were created (:30). Look for answers to Moses' questions in verses 31-42. What did you learn about how the world and its inhabitants were created? What did you learn about why they were created? What additional questions do you have after reading God's response? How many of those questions can be answered by verse 35?

God used the phrases "innumerable" and "cannot be numbered" to describe His creations, and yet He also declared that those things are "numbered unto me, for they are mine" (:35, and 37). Why do you think it is important to know that God knows, numbers, and is aware of all His creations?

Verse 39 is one of the most important verses about God in all of scripture. It is the most quoted scripture of all time in General Conference. Immortality means that a person can live forever, and eternal life means to live like God. What is important about the phrase "work and glory"? What would happen if God ever quit or retired? How does this verse become even more significant if we change the last word to say, "His family" or your own name?

Day 5, Moses 2 and Genesis 1

When it comes to the creation of the world, it is very helpful to remember what the Lord said will come to pass in the Millennium (D&C 101:32-33). We do not yet know everything about how the world was created, nor all the purposes. We don't need to worry about our faith flying to pieces when we study what science must teach us. We can have a testimony in both rock and book.

As you study Genesis 1, look for and mark the word "God." In Moses 2, mark the words "I" and "I God." When you are done with this assignment, it will become abundantly clear that although we may not know everything about how the earth was made, it is totally clear who made it. Why is it important for us to know that we are not cosmic accidents?

Another phrase that is repeated often in these two chapters is "after his kind" or "after their kind." Each creation that reproduced does so after their kind. This is important because verses 26-27—regardless of which chapter you are reading—teach us about whom we are created after. How does knowing that we are created in the image of God change how we think about ourselves and about God?

What instruction did God give to mankind in verses 27-29? How well are we doing at these responsibilities? Is there any counsel in these verses that you think is being misunderstood?

Day 6, Moses 3

What can we learn about the purpose of the Sabbath day from its creation in verses 1-3?

The following quote from Joseph Fielding Smith helps to dismiss much of the confusion that people often experience when studying the Fall. After reading verses 16-17 he said, "Now this is the way I interpret that: The Lord said to Adam, here is the tree of the knowledge of good and evil. If you want to stay here, then you cannot eat of that fruit. If you want to stay here, then I forbid you to eat it. But you may act for yourself, and you may eat of it if you want to. And if you eat it, you will die. I see a great difference between transgressing the law and committing a sin" (Joseph Fielding Smith, "Fall-Atonement-Resurrection-Sacrament," in Charge to Religious Educators, p. 124, as quoted in Doctrines of the Gospel Student Manual Religion 430 and 431 p. 20).

They could eat of every tree, but one of these trees had a condition placed upon it, if they ate from it. It was not forbidden to eat of it. It was forbidden to eat of it and stay in the garden after eating of it. Adding these phrases and words to the language of the scriptures helps make this clear. If God didn't want them to partake of that tree, He would not have put it in the "midst" of the garden, where Adam and Eve had to pass by it anytime they went anywhere (:9).

What can we learn about marriage from Adam and Eve in verses 18-25?

Day 7, Moses 4:1-14

What can you learn about Satan, Christ, and the pre-mortal life from verses 1-4?

In verse 4 we learn that Satan was the "father of all lies." As you study verses 5-11, look for the lies that he tells Eve. Why do you think he told half-truths? In what ways, does Satan continue to use half-truths to confuse and beguile people today?

Look for reasons that Eve and Adam partook of the fruit in verse 12. How do you think they felt in verses 13 and 14? Why do we try to hide our actions from God? Having God find them, and us, is the best thing that can happen, but we hide. Is there anything in your life that you are trying to hide from God?

Day 8, Moses 4:15-32

Having caught Adam and Eve in their attempt to hide, God asks several questions in verses 15-19 to help them learn from their experience. What do you love about God's parenting strategy?

Remember to add the words "and stay in the garden" after "whereof I commanded thee that thou shouldn't not eat" (:17). This helps with the confusion.

In verse 18, Adam is often accused of throwing Eve "under the bus," but what he is doing is telling us about the commandment to remain with Eve. Adam knew that she would have to leave the garden after partaking of the fruit. Adam, in an act of faith and love, partook of the fruit, choosing to stay with Eve rather than to remain alone. There are great lessons of commitment and companionship in this often-misused scripture.

In verses 20-25, look for what the consequences of the Fall were for Satan, Eve, and Adam.

How is verse 21 a wonderful prophecy about Jesus' power and eventual victory over Satan?

The wording of Adam ruling over his wife in verse 22 could be troubling if we had not been taught that to "rule," in this instance, is to preside, and to "preside" is to lead as the Savior did (D&C 121:34-46).

There is a marvelous amount of Atonement symbolism in the clothing of Adam and Eve in verse 27. What symbols can you see?

Many in the world wrongly believe the Fall was a negative thing. Look for God's own opinion about Adam and Eve after the Fall in verse 28.

Day 9, Moses 5:1-11

What additional lessons about marriage can you learn from verses 1-4?

Partaking of the fruit was not of great concern to God; it was that Adam and Eve had done so at the bidding of Satan (D&C 29:40). God then gives a commandment, without explanation, to Adam and Eve to sacrifice the firstlings of their flocks. We know this was to improve and teach obedience. Look in verses 5-6 to see how well they learned the lesson. Why do you think willing obedience is an important, even an essential law that God's people must master?

In verses 7-9 we get an explanation from an angel and the Holy Ghost about how an animal sacrifice is a symbol of Christ. How much more personal do you think this symbolism was in its meaning to Adam and Eve, who had named and lived with these animals that now had to die because of Adam and Eve's choice?

Look in verses 10-11 to discover what Adam and Eve learned from the Fall and the Atonement. What was the difference between Adam's and Eve's perspectives?

Day 10, Moses 5:12-31

Surely the children of Adam and Eve would have certain advantages in the development of their spirituality. Think of the testimony, stories, and experiences that Adam and Eve could share with them. Look for what Adam and Eve experienced as parents in verses 12-16. What would happen to us if the Holy Ghost stopped correcting us?

Today we are going to discover some of the things that caused Cain, who was raised by righteous parents, to reject the gospel and even become Perdition. As you study verses 16-31, identify the following attitudes Cain had, which led to his spiritual death.

- :16 He was not concerned about spiritual things.
- :18 He loved Satan's praise and acceptance more than God's.
- :19 Sacred ordinances were not significant or important to him.
- :21 He became angry when his pitiful spiritual attempts were not accepted and rewarded like the significant efforts of others.
- :23-26 He refused to listen to the warnings and corrections of God and the prophets because of anger.
- :28 He found others who felt as he did and spent his time with them.

- :29-31 He made covenants with Satan to get what he wanted, no matter who it hurt.

Do you ever find yourself or your loved ones in possession of any of these dangerous attitudes?

Day 11, Moses 5:32-59

Yesterday we explored several attitudes that led Cain toward the choice of perdition. As you study verses 32-41, identify the following attitudes that led to Cain's spiritual decline.

- :33 He rejoiced and celebrated his wicked choices and boasted of their benefits.
- :34 He lied to cover up what he had done and didn't care about anyone but himself.
- :38 When caught, he refused to be accountable and blamed others for his actions.
- :39 His remorse was based on fear of what would happen when others found out what he had done. He did not have sorrow for how his actions caused pain to others and to God.
- :41 He was shut out of God's presence and then takes others with him.

What will you do to be more watchful and repentant of these attitudes that we have studied the last two days?

In verse 40 notice that the mark placed on Cain, whatever it was, was placed as an act of love and mercy from God, and not a curse. The curse was being shut out of God's presence.

Verses 42-59 mention several of Cain's decedents who also made choices that led to them being cursed rather than accepting preaching, angels, and holy ordinances.

Day 12, Moses 6:1-25

As you study verses 1-25, look for what Adam, Eve, and their decedents did to teach their children and others the gospel. What can we learn from their example about the responsibility parents should teach their children?

What parents do you know, yours or others, that really do this well? What ideas and feelings have you had as you have studied today about how to do this now or in the future?

Complete this statement after reading verse 15: "Adam, Eve, and their children sought to build faith and families. Satan seeks to . . ."

Day 13, Moses 6:26-47

Enoch is called to go on a mission to a people for whom God has prepared a hell "if they repent not" (:29). Look in verses 27-29 for the things that would create misery in someone' life or cause him or her to go to hell or spirit prison. These people are making terrible choices, and yet God calls His servants to minister to them. Why is it important to know that the Lord doesn't want people who are living hellish lives to go to hell?

Ponder on these two questions:

When have you felt like you were not good enough?

When have you felt like you had a weakness that kept you from doing something the Lord had asked you to do?

Look in verse 31 for the concerns Enoch had when the Lord called him. What promises did the Lord make to Enoch in verses 32-34 and what did Enoch have to do to get those promises? What does this teach us about how the Lord looks on weak, incapable, or inadequate people?

In verses 35-36, Enoch became a seer, and was now able to see things that other mortals could not see. In verses 37-47, look for what Enoch taught and how the people reacted to him. In verse 38, the people called Enoch a "wild man." Who are our wild men, or seers, today? How does the world treat them? Do you think they feel or felt like Enoch did? What types of things are the prophets seeing and warning us about that people may not see clearly now?

Day 14, Moses 6:48-68

Read verse 48 and then finish this phrase: "Because of the Fall there is . . ."

We have two options in how to respond to the Fall. Satan's offer is found in verse 49 and God's offer is in verses 50-52. Which of those is the most appealing to you?

Upon hearing God's option, Enoch records that Adam asked why people had to repent and be baptized (:53). As requested by Adam, God provided answers to both questions. In verses 54-57, look for why people must repent. Then, in verses 58-59, look for reasons why people must be baptized. How would you summarize what you learned from God's answers to Adam's question?

In verse 60, the word "justified" means to be pardoned from punishment, and "sanctified" means that one is made clean and holy. In verse 61, we learn a life-changing lesson. According to verse 61, how do people know if they are justified and sanctified through the Atonement? Verse 62 then declares that what we have been taught in verses 48-61 is the "plan of salvation unto all men, through the blood of mine Only Begotten."

Verse 63 is the foundation for every object lesson. Start pondering about this verse and you will start getting inspired thoughts and feelings. Expect God to teach you incredible truths about the Atonement in unexpected ways and at unexpected times.

Verses 64-68 cover the baptism and confirmation of Adam. What do you find intriguing bout this account?

Day 15, Moses 7:1-21

Verses 1-12 contain some of Enoch's prophesying and preaching. What miracle in verses 13-15 do you think is the most remarkable?

While there was fighting among all the people of the earth, look in verses 16-21 for what Enoch and his people did to establish righteousness. Did you notice that before you can build a righteous city, you first must build a righteous people (:18-19)? Verse 18 is the instruction for building a people and a city that were so righteous that they were taken up into heaven. What are the key truths in that verse that could make you, your family, and your city more Godlike? When have you seen an individual, a family, a ward, or a city live those same principles?

In verse 21 we learn that "Zion, in process of time was taken up into heaven." In verse 68, we learn how long that took. How can that fact help keep us from getting discouraged about our progress?

Day 16, Moses 7:22-40

This is one of the most important sections of scripture for comparing the characters of Satan and God. With the departure of Zion and other righteous people being caught up to Zion, Satan's power spread over the earth. Look for how Satan and God responded to this increasing darkness in verses 23-38. Confused about how one as great as God could be weeping, Enoch asks several times for God to explain why He weeps in verses 28-31. What were the reasons that Enoch gave for why he thought God should not be weeping?

In response to Enoch's questions, God explains with tremendous vulnerability about why He weeps in verses 32-40. What does God's answer reveal about what He wants most from His children? How can these verses that you have studied today change our understanding of just how great our God really is? How does your love, faith, and desire to do good increase because of a weeping God?

What will you do or not do so that God rejoices rather than weeps today? What will you do or not do so that Satan has no opportunity to laugh today?

Day 17, Moses 7:41-58

In yesterday's section, we saw and learned of the reasons why God weeps. As you study verses 41-58, look for who else starts to weep. What are the reasons given for their weeping?

Look for how each question Enoch asks allows him to get more and more revelation and understanding. What questions will you ask of God today to allow you to get more and more revelation and understanding?

When Enoch refused to be comforted, the Lord asked him to "Lift up your heart, and be glad, and look" (:44). What did the Lord show Enoch in verses 45-47 that caused Enoch's soul to rejoice? How can the things Enoch saw also cause our souls to rejoice?

What fantastic promises did the Lord give in verses 53?

Day 18, Moses 7:59-69

In Moses 7:4, the Lord told Enoch that He would show him many events in the history of the world. Enoch saw the building and taking-up of Zion, the

Flood of the wicked, the Atonement of Jesus Christ, and, in verses 59-62, he saw the Second Coming of Jesus Christ. In verse 61, we read that there will be great tribulation and destruction before the Second Coming, but the Lord promised to preserve His people. How will He do that? How will He preserve His people? His answer is found in verse 62. The "righteousness" that will be sent down from heaven is revelation (:62). The "truth" that will "come forth from out of the earth, to bear testimony" of Christ's resurrection, to sweep and flood the earth to gather the elect, is the Book of Mormon (:62). Have you allowed the Book of Mormon and the words of living prophets to flood and sweep over you, causing you to both gather and gird (:62)?

In verse 63, Enoch saw the return of his Zion, coming down from heaven and joining with the New Jerusalem that is yet to be built. What do you love about how these two holy cities greeted each other? Is it possible for that kind of love to bear sway now?

Look in verses 64-65 and 67 to see what else God showed Enoch.

In verse 66 we learn that, before the Second Coming, the hearts of men and women will fail them, and with fear they look forward to the coming judgment. They are fearful because they have not relied on the scriptures and the words of the prophets.

Day 19, Moses 8

In verses 1-12, we get the generations from Enoch to Noah's sons. In verses 11-15, we see that there are the "sons of God," or the covenant, and the "sons of men." God said that the daughters of God had sold themselves because they married the sons of men outside of the covenant.

In verse 18, the word "giant" is used. In Genesis 6:4, the Hebrew word for giant is *nĕphiyl* which means a bully, tyrant, feller, or one who falls or apostatized (see Strong's Concordance H5303). In Moses 8:16-26 and 28-30, look for what these rebellious people were doing at the time of Noah.

Why do you think they would want to kill a prophet of God? What similarities do you see between the conditions of Noah's day and ours? How long did the Lord give them to repent in verse 17? What does that teach you about God's patience? What principle can we learn from these people's refusal to repent? Do you view repentance as a blessing or a burden?

How did Noah and his sons respond to the Lord in verse 27? D&C 76:69 says that just men are "made perfect" through Jesus' Atonement.

Day 20, Genesis 6

Having completed the Joseph Smith Translation of Genesis 1-5 in Moses 1-8, we will now move our study to Genesis 6. Verses 1-13 were covered in Moses 8. Because of the violence and sin mentioned in verses 11-13, God gave Noah instruction on how to save his family. As you read this saving instruction to Noah in verses 14-21, consider what saving instruction God has given to you and your family. Then, notice how Noah responded to such instruction in verse 22. Is there any important personal instruction that you have received from God for your family that you have been putting off or delaying?

In verse 14, Noah is told to pitch the ark within and without. The Hebrew word for pitch is *kopher* (Strong's H3724), and it comes from the root word *kaphar* (Strong's H3722), which means to cover, reconcile, or make an atonement. This is the word used 71 times to speak of what the Atonement does for us. The pitch or tar used to make the ark waterproof is a symbol of how the Atonement can protect us. There are some things that should stay out of our lives, and some things that should stay in, and only by being completely covered outwardly and inwardly are we safe.

Footnote 16a provides a wonderful connection to Noah's boat-building counterpart in the Book of Mormon, the Brother of Jared.

Because of the wickedness of the world, God gave instruction on how to build an ark. As you read verses 18-19, replace the word "ark" with "temple," and see if the content now fits the context of our day.

Day 21, Genesis 7

This chapter begins and ends with Noah and his family safely in the ark. The whole flood story can be seen as evidence of how far God will go to save one righteous family. In the last days, we are told that wickedness will again prevail to the point that God will again be willing to save His righteous families through the destruction of the wicked by fire (1 Nephi 22:16-17).

Many prophets have identified the flood as a symbol of baptism and the destruction of fire at the Second Coming as a symbol of the earth receiving the Holy Ghost. What do these symbols teach you about the importance these ordinances can have?

The destruction in verses 21-23 seem at odds with other scriptures that we know about God (2 Nephi 26:24, 30; and Moses 1:39). Elder Neal A. Maxwell, of the Quorum of the Twelve Apostles, explained that God intervened "when corruption had reached an agency-destroying point that spirits could not, in justice, be sent here" (*We Will Prove Them Herewith* [1982], 58). President John Taylor explained that "by taking away their earthly existence [God] prevented them from entailing their sins upon their posterity and degenerating [or corrupting] them, and also prevented them from committing further acts of wickedness" ("Discourse Delivered by President John Taylor," Deseret News, Jan. 16, 1878, 787). According to these quotes, how was the flood an act of mercy and love, or for the benefit of people?

Day 22, Genesis 8-9

We are already familiar with the Joseph Smith Translation of the Bible because of the book of Moses. In the chapters that you will study today, you will see both JST footnotes and the JST Appendix. Not all of the Joseph Smith Translation is included in the LDS edition of the scriptures. The changes that were of doctrinal significance or important for clarification were put in the footnotes, like Genesis 9:9a, 11c, 15a, and 26a. Larger portions were included in the Appendix, like Genesis 9:4-6, 11-14, and 21-25. In digital format, you can access the Appendix by clicking on the footnotes or going to the Joseph Smith Translation in the Scripture section.

As you examine the sections in the JST Appendix and footnotes, look for the promises and covenants that God made to Noah and Enoch. Look for what God said about the importance of life, including animal life. Also look for the symbolic meaning that God placed upon the rainbow.

The story in Genesis 9:18-27 often causes confusion because Noah, a prophet, gets drunk and Ham sees the nakedness of his father and is cursed. This story is not fully understood, but here are some helpful ideas. The ancient prophets didn't have our modern Word of Wisdom, but drinking to the point of intoxication is disapproved by God. Many scholars retranslate the word "nakedness" to mean "skin covering," like that given to Adam and Eve. Many even teach that Ham was trying to obtain this garment to claim priesthood power, and that is what brought on the curse. The wording of JST Genesis 9:26a was used in the past to justify priesthood restriction based upon race. In the 2013 edition of the LDS scriptures, the introduction to Official Declaration 2 in the D&C states that there are "no clear insights into the origins of this practice" of priesthood restriction because of race.

Day 23, Genesis 10-11

These chapters are almost completely of a genealogical nature, except for the story of the Tower of Babel. In Genesis 10:8-9; 11:1-9, look for what we can learn about those who came up with the idea. How did the Lord respond?

Here are some reasons why they may have built the tower:

- They wanted to be able to do whatever they wished and still make it to heaven.
- They wanted to have a way to escape if God ever punished their wickedness with a flood again.
- They wanted to have a place for false temple worship.
- They wanted to get high enough for Nimrod to shoot an arrow into heaven and kill God.

What problems or misunderstandings did these people have? Do we have the same problems or misunderstandings today?

How was the tower they were building different than the temples of God? If you had a friend in the Tower of Babel, what would you say to them to try to get them to the temple? A former student and dear friend of mine, Marcus Jensen, said: "Why would anyone go to the world or the Tower of Babel instead of the temple? It offers you nothing." What do you feel makes the difference between going to the Tower of Babel or to the temple?

Day 24, Translation and Historicity of the Book of Abraham

The reading for today's section is found under the Church History icon on your Gospel Library app. Then click on Gospel Topic Essays. You can also find this essay on LDS.org. As you study, consider the following questions.

What did you learn about the origins and translation of the Book of Abraham?

What did this article teach you about the relationship between the small amounts of fragments that were found in 1966 and the Book of Abraham?

Why have some people been troubled because of the fragments of the papyri that were recovered? In what ways are the Book of Abraham and the missing, lost, or burned papyri like the Book of Mormon and the Gold Plates?

What are some of the things mentioned in the article that are found in the text of the Book of Abraham and would indicate it is an ancient and authentic work?

Day 25, Abraham 1:1-11

Abraham is my hero because he was righteous in circumstances where many would not be righteous. Nothing about his culture or family was motivating him to be righteous, only his own commitment. If you come from a community or family that does not support or encourage you to be faithful to God and His commands, then Abraham is your example.

In verses 1-2, look for what things Abraham desired and sought. You may want to make a list of each. Because Abraham sought and desired these things, he received them in verses 3-4. What are the things for which you desire and seek? Chances are you will obtain them, good or bad.

As you search verses 5-11, look for other things that made it difficult for Abraham or others in his area choose to be righteous. In what kind of circumstances did they live? From the example of Abraham and the three daughters of Onitah, what do you feel we can learn? Can you be righteous in difficult circumstances like high school, buses, locker rooms, cabins, campouts, college, jobs, sports, parties, and dances? Can you be Abraham? Will you be Abraham?

Day 26, Abraham 1:12-27

Abraham is the only book of scripture that has pictures. These pictures are called facsimiles, and are copies of the original pictures. The first one depicts the events from verses 12-20 and is not just a traditional lion couch scene from Egyptology. How did Abraham get free? What promises were made to him? Why doesn't God always provide such miraculous savings? What thoughts and feelings do you think this event caused when God asked Abraham to sacrifice his own son years later?

Verses 21-27 address the establishment of Egypt and Pharaoh. They have been used in many ways to justify priesthood restriction based on race. After the 1978 revelation lifting the priesthood and temple ban, Elder Bruce R. McConkie, said the following to the teachers in the Church Education System: "Forget everything that I have said, or what President Brigham Young or President George Q. Cannon or whomsoever has said in days past that is contrary to the present revelation. We spoke with a limited understanding and without the light and knowledge that now has come into the world." ("All Are Alike unto God." CES Religious Educators Symposium on 18 August 1978). There have always been restrictions on the priesthood until now. You live in the time when any worthy male may hold the priesthood. What does that teach you about the time in which you now live?

Day 27, Abraham 1:28-2:13

In Abraham 1:28-2:5, look for how the members of the family reacted when there was famine and when there was plenty. How have your hardships helped to turn you to God? Why might it be harder to turn to God when times are prosperous?

Abraham 2:6-11 is the best place in all of scripture to study the Abrahamic Covenant. As you study, look for the blessings the Lord promised to Abraham and the responsibilities that Abraham assumed. These blessings and responsibilities also rest upon everyone who has entered a covenant of baptism (Galatians 3:26-29). What actions have you taken to fulfill these responsibilities, so that you might inherit the promised blessings? In what ways have these responsibilities and blessings helped to shape the direction of your life?

In verses 12-13, you will find the following idea: Those who seek God's will find Him, and He will provide deliverance and instruction.

Day 28, Abraham 2:14-25 and Genesis 12:14-20

Abraham is a splendid example in all things. In Abraham 2:14-20, we get to see what this great man and his family are like on the road as they travel—almost like a modern-day vacation setting. Note the various places they went and how they built altars for sacrifice. These sacrifices are equivalent to us partaking of the sacrament. Did Abraham change who he was when he traveled? What do these actions of Abraham teach us about what is important to him?

Because Abraham was willing to be obedient to whatever God commanded, God could both protect and prosper him. In Abraham 2:21-25 and Genesis 12:14-20, look for how God protected and prospered Abraham and Sarai as they were obedient. How has God both protected and prospered you recently?

Day 29, Abraham 3:1-21

In the Church, we sing the hymn "If You Could Hie to Kolob." Seminary students love this hymn. It causes them to think about spiritually deep and significant things. Kolob is one of the endless created worlds of our Heavenly Father. Kolob is of importance because it is symbolic of Jesus Christ and His leadership. Therefore, as you learn about Kolob in verses 1-17 and in the lyrics of the hymn, you are learning about Jesus Christ and His ways of living and leading. What eternal truth did you learn this time?

Abraham was shown all the stars of heaven so that when God promised him that his seed would be like those stars, Abraham could comprehend the significance of the promise (:12-14). Only those who become like Heavenly Father and Heavenly Mother get to have posterity like the sands of the seashore and the stars. Are you seeing the big picture like Abraham yet?

In verses 6, 8, 16, 17, 18, and 19 there is a similar phrase, thought, and fact: All things are not equal; one is often above another. Abraham was shown this in the stars so that he might understand it when it came to spirits. Although we have existed as long as God, we have not advanced like He has (:18-21). One of the greatest things about God is that He desires us, because of love, to rise and become like Him, so that we might enjoy what He enjoys. Tomorrow we will learn how He planned to do this.

Day 30, Abraham 3:22-28

God transitioned from showing Abraham all His creations to showing Abraham about himself. What did God show Abraham about himself in verses 22-23? Was there anything said of Abraham that could not also be said of you? What significant responsibilities in this life do you believe were placed upon you?

In verse 24 we learn that Jesus Christ, with the help of the noble and great ones, created an earth as part of Heavenly Father's plan. According to verse 25, what is the great test or proof of life? This proving and testing began in the premortal life, or "first estate." What was promised in verse 26 to those who prove themselves faithful in the first and second estates? When have you felt that you have become more like God in how you think, feel, and act when you have done what He has asked? Experiences like that are evidence that you are having glory added upon you.

Verses 27-28 are about Jesus Christ, the greater star, and Satan, the fallen star. What will you do to make sure that anger and jealously don't rob you of opportunities to have glory added upon you today?

Day 31, Abraham 4

This chapter adds tremendous insight to our understanding of the creation. To which part of the creation does this chapter refer, according to the heading? Why is this an important aspect of all great accomplishments?

As you study this chapter, you may want to mark the following words as they occur and then ponder about the significance they add: "Gods," "organize/organized," "ordered," and "prepare/prepared."

This chapter destroys the idea that God created things *ex nihilo*, or "out of nothing. There was matter, organizing, and even obeying (:10, 12, 18, 21, and 25). Because the creation would deal with the coupling of eternal elements with mortal matter, there had to be choice on the part of all things organized. That is why King Benjamin mentioned that we are not as faithful as the dust of the earth (Mosiah 2:22-26). Enjoy being dust-like in your humble obedience today.

Day 32, Abraham 5

In verses 1-3, we learn that this beautiful earth was the result of a heavenly council. Counseling, if done right, is a means to produce and create powerful results and miracles. What miracles have you seen come forth from counseling with others?

Remember what we learned about the tree of good and evil from the quote on day six.

What do you think the symbolism of creating Eve from the rib of Adam means? What would a bone taken from the foot or head have symbolized? Does verse 18 help us to understand this better?

In verses 20-21, we learn that each animal received its name from Adam. How does that make the command to sacrifice some of them more painful and instructive in its symbolism of Christ?

Day 33, Genesis 13

In verses 1-7, look for what problem developed between the herdsmen of Lot and Abram. What solution to this problem did Abram propose in verses 8-9? What would happen if everyone lived verse 8 in their relationships? Abram didn't care about stuff, only about the relationships and making sure there was no strife.

In verses 10-18, look for why Lot selected the land that he did. Where did he pitch his tent (:13)? Why do you think Lot pitched his tent toward a people who acted like they did in verse 14? What did the Lord promise Abram with the land he was going to receive? What did Abram do when he got to his new land? Is your household pointed toward Sodom or toward altars? Is your goal of life to increase your wealth and pleasure or to improve and protect relationships?

Day 34, Genesis 14

In verses 1-12, we see the political unrest and warring of many kings. During these battles, Lot, Abram's nephew, was taken captive along with the goods of Sodom and Gomorrah. In the last chapter, Lot pitched his tent toward Sodom (Genesis 13:12). In Genesis 14:12, we learn that Lot was living in Sodom. What can this fact teach us about the danger of drift? Are there any ideas, beliefs, or morals on which you have drifted? Are there things that you used to look upon with a curiosity that you now embrace without question or consideration?

In verses 13-16, Abram gathered his servants and went to rescue Lot. To be like Abram, we must rescue our friends and family. Which family member or friend do you know that needs to be rescued?

Following Abram's great victory, two kings called upon him to pay their respects. What are the differences you see between these two kings in verses 17-21? Why didn't Abram take the great wealth that the king of Sodom was offering (:21-23)? What threads and shoelaces of wickedness do the popular of the world keep offering to you in an attempt to get you to break your covenant?

Day 35, Genesis 14:24a or JST Genesis 14:15-40

What do these inspired verses teach us about Melchizedek and the priesthood that bears his name?

What are some of the impressive miracles that were performed by faith and priesthood in these verses? This list of miracles is large. What miracles, from your life, could you add to the list?

In D&C 107:1-4, we learn that the Melchizedek Priesthood was named after Melchizedek because of his notable example and his symbolism of Christ. What symbols of Christ did you see in the behavior and actions of Melchizedek in today's verses?

Day 36, Genesis 15

In verse 1, God declared to Abram that He would be his "shield" and his "exceeding great reward." How has God protected and shielded you from danger and the world this week?

In verses 2-7, God and Abram discussed children and property. The only people that are promised to have children like the stars of heaven are those who will become like our Heavenly Parents (:5; D&C 132:30-32). In addition to God showing Abram the stars, Abram was also allowed to see the coming of Christ (:6a, or JST Genesis 15:9-12).

When Abram asked for evidence from God that the promises of posterity and property would be fulfilled, God had Abram take several animals cut them in half, and place them on the ground opposite each other. While awaiting the arrival of the Lord, Abram shooed away birds from the carcasses, and was tormented by a dream of darkness and horror about his posterity being enslaved and later delivered from Egypt (:10-16). In verses 17-21, the Lord appears to Abram, symbolized as a "smoking furnace, and a burning lamp" — we might say something like a pillar of fire. The Lord then passes between the divided animals, symbolizing that if God doesn't keep His covenant to Abram regarding posterity and property that He, God, would be divided and destroyed like the animals which He walked through. With every covenant that people make with God, He places Himself on the line, promising His own destruction if He does not fulfill His part. What does this incredible story teach you about the sacredness, power, and commitment we have through our covenants with God?

Day 37, Genesis 16

Search verses 1-6 for all the places where hard feelings or offences could have occurred.

In verses 7-10, look for what God did to help Hagar in this moment of pain and anger. Why might the instruction given to Hagar have been hard counsel to follow? If she doesn't go back, she and her son will not be blessed, and they are to play an distinguished role in Islam. Those who are offended and leave the Church don't get the blessings unless they come back.

Look at the meaning of the names that Hagar gave to her son, Ishmael, and the well (:11a, and 14b). Hagar learned from this experience that God hears, sees, weeps with, and cares for His children through all their offences. Complete the following statement: "When I get, my feelings hurt by a member of the Church or by a Church leader I should remember…"

Day 38, Genesis 17

Look for how tough the commandment is that God gave to Abram in verse 1. To be perfect doesn't mean that a person has never sinned; it means that they have reached a point where they stop sinning. Verses 2-9 repeat the Abrahamic covenant that we studied earlier.

Footnotes 3a and 7a take you to the JST Appendix and add a tremendous amount of information and doctrine to the text. As you read these JST portions, look for what they say about baptism, Abel, circumcision, and accountability. How did the JST verses help you to understand why God commanded the law of circumcision in Genesis 17:10-14? What do you love about how quickly Abraham responded to the commandment to perform circumcision in verses 23-27?

Whenever we make significant covenants with God, we also receive names. Abram, whose name means "exalted father," had his name changed to Abraham, which means "father of multitudes" (:5). Sarai, which means "princess of her own people," had her name changed to Sarah, which means "princess of all people" (:15). What names have you received in association with the covenants that you have made with God? What is the significance of each of these name changes?

God promised Abraham and Sarah that they will have a son, and that through him, not Ishmael, the covenant will continue (:19).

Day 39, Genesis 18

In verses 1-8, look for how Abraham sought to take care of some strangers, who turned out to be holy men. How are those in need and the prophets treated inside of your home?

Because of the hospitality and kindness, the holy men left a blessing upon Abraham and Sarah in verses 9-13. What was the blessing, and how did Sara respond? In response to Sarah and all of us, the Lord asked a question in verse 14. How would you answer the Lord's question? What impossible things have you experienced?

The next day, the holy men arose and headed for Sodom. In verses 17-19, the Lord said He would reveal unto Abraham what would happen to Sodom, because of Abraham's character as a man and father. Can the Lord trust you enough to tell and whisper things to you through the Holy Ghost?

In verses 20-33, Abraham learned of the destruction of Sodom and talked to the Lord about saving the city if there is 50, 45, 30, 20, and finally 10 righteous people in the city. The righteous, in many cases, protect the wicked from destruction. Do you have friends and family that are better protected from making bad choices when you are around? Do you have friends and family that cause you to be better protected because of their presence?

Day 40, Genesis 19

In verses 1-16, notice how Lot, the Men of Sodom, and Lot's family reacted to and treated the holy men and their message. Compare what you find with Abraham in Genesis 18. Footnotes 1a, 5a, 8a, and 12a are essential to understand the full measure of this story.

Verses 17-29 contain the escape of Lot and his family from Sodom, the warning counsel not to look behind, and Lot's wife ignoring that counsel. Elder Jeffrey R. Holland gave a great insight on this story when he said: "I plead with you not to dwell on days now gone, nor to yearn vainly for yesterdays, however good those yesterdays may have been. The past is to be learned from but not lived in. We look back to claim the embers from glowing experiences but not the ashes. And when we have learned what we need to learn and have brought with us the best that we have experienced, then we look ahead, we remember that faith is always pointed toward the future. Faith always has to do with blessings and truths and events that will yet be efficacious in our lives. So, a more theological way to talk about Lot's wife is to say that she did not have faith. She doubted the Lord's ability to give her something better than she already had. Apparently, she thought—fatally, as it turned out—that nothing that lay ahead could possibly be as good as those moments she was leaving behind" (Jeffrey R. Holland. "Remember Lot's Wife" [Brigham Young University devotional address, Jan. 13, 2009], 2–3; speeches.byu.edu).

The story in verses 30-38 is disturbing. I have a good friend who said of this story "You can take the children out of Sodom, but you can't take Sodom out of the children." How does this story and quote influence you regarding choices that you will make that could impact your children?

Day 41, Genesis 20

In verses 1-2, Sarah was taken by king Abimalech. In verses 3-7, look for who warned Abimalech and how he was warned before he commited bigger sins. President Boyd K. Packer said: "No member of this Church—and that means each of you—will ever make a serious mistake without first being warned by the promptings of the Holy Ghost. Sometimes when you have made a mistake, you may have said afterward, 'I knew I should not have done that. It did not feel right,' or perhaps, 'I knew I should have done that. I just did not have the courage to act!' Those impressions are the Holy Ghost attempting to direct you toward good or warning you away from harm" (Boyd K. Packer. "How to Survive in Enemy Territory," New Era, Apr. 2012, 3). When have you, like Abimalech, received a warning that what you were doing was wrong so you could be protected? Will you be attentive to that voice today, so that if He needs to warn you, you will be listening and ready to act?

In verses 8-18, look for how Abimalech repented and how Abraham healed Abimalech's household. How long must Sarah have been with Abimalech for his household to need the drastic healing found in verses 17-18?

In verse 12, Abraham explained more about how Sarah was his sister through his father, but not his mother. This still grosses people out, but remember that back then they had fewer options for marrying in the covenant. Thank goodness there are millions of members in the Church today, so our dating, and marriage options are expanded.

Day 42, Genesis 21

In verses 1-8, look for how God, Abraham, and Sarah all kept their covenants. Abraham and Sarah have waited decades for this event to happen. What can this teach us about having patience with God and His covenants and promises? In what ways has God's keeping of His promises and covenants caused you to both laugh and rejoice (:6a)?

In verse 9, Sarah saw Ishmael mocking. Note how Sarah responded in verse 10. Abraham's feelings are described in verse 11. The Lord's response to the whole thing is found in verses 12-13.

As you read the heart-rending words of verses 14-21, look for evidence that God did not abandon Hagar and Ishmael. When was a time that you were in the midst of an affliction and God opened your eyes, so you could see Him blessing you (:19)?

Day 43, Genesis 22

God's requirement of Abraham to sacrifice his son Isaac can cause disturbing thoughts. There ae two scriptures to help us make sense of the sacrifice of Isaac: D&C 101:4-5 and Jacob 4:4-5.

In Genesis 22:5, Abraham told his servants that he "and the lad will go yonder and worship." By "worship," he meant sacrifice his son. Thus, we learn that at the root of all worship is sacrifice. Elder Neal A. Maxwell said: "Real, personal sacrifice never was placing an animal on the altar. Instead, it is a willingness to put the animal in us upon the altar and letting it be consumed!" (Neal A. Maxwell. "Deny Yourselves of All Ungodliness," *Ensign*, May 1995, p. 68). Joseph Smith said: "A religion that does not require the sacrifice of all things never has power sufficient to produce the faith necessary unto life and salvation; for, from the first existence of man, the faith necessary unto the enjoyment of life and salvation never could be obtained without the sacrifice of all earthly things" (Joseph Smith, *Lectures on Faith*, 6:7).

From what you have read in D&C 101:4-5 and the quotes above, why does God require his people to sacrifice or worship?

In Jacob 4:4-5 we learn that Abraham is a symbol of Heavenly Father and that Isaac is a symbol of Jesus Christ. How does the story in Genesis 22 enhance your appreciation for what Heavenly Father and Jesus Christ went through to complete the Atonement? For the rest of us there is a ram in the thicket, which can be offered in our stead, but not for the Father or the Son.

Day 44, Genesis 23-24

Read the chapter heading for Genesis 23.

When I have faith, I will trust in the Lord and act. Look for and list how the following people in Genesis 25 demonstrated amazing faith:

- Abraham
- The servant
- Rebekah
- Rebekah's family
- Isaac

With which example of faith were you the most impressed? Will you practice having more faith in God, covenants, and miracles?

Day 45, Genesis 25

In verses 1-19, we will see new additions to the family of Abraham, then his death and burial by Isaac and Ishmael. Through the children of Ishmael we finally start to see the promise begin to be fulfilled, that nations would through Abraham. The rest of the Bible is about how this promise was also fulfilled through Isaac.

What do you find fascinating about the birth story in verses 20-26? What does this story teach us about the spirituality of righteous mothers? Notice how long it took for these intense prayers to be answered. What feelings do you have when a 20-year prayer is answered? Do you have a problem or issue in your life that may take 20 years before your prayers are answered?

In what ways is the story in verses 27-34 a reminder not to give up eternal blessings for momentary pleasure? What other sins or struggles do you think Esau might have had if he had a difficulty choosing the eternal when the temporal pleasure was strong? Do you think he might struggle with tithing, family prayer and scripture study, schoolwork, dating standards, personal prayer and scripture study, electronic devices during sacrament or classes, pornography, and work or school over mission? What momentary pleasures will be offered to you today in exchange for your eternal blessings?

Day 46, Genesis 26

In verses 1-6, the Lord renews the Abrahamic Covenant with Isaac. Then, in verses 7-11, Isaac and Rebekah pulled the whole "She's my sister, so don't kill me" thing.

In verses 12-33, look for how many times Isaac and his servants moved and dug wells so that they don't have strife and arguments. In the middle of this war-for-wells, the Lord appeared to Isaac in verse 24 and told him to "fear not, for I am with thee." Why do you think we forget that God wants to help us? Isaac balanced his life with worship, home and family, and work (building alters, pitching tents, and digging wells). Why is it important to have a good balance of these things? How is your balance of worship, home and family, and work? Isaac was very patient with those fighting for his wells. Do you think he was as patient with the wars inside his own tent?

What did Esau do in verse 34 that caused grief to Isaac and Rebekah in verse 35? What does their grief teach you about the importance of that sacred ordinance?

Day 47, Genesis 27

As you read this chapter, use the following quotes and sayings.

Sister Julie B. Beck said of Rebekah: "She needed to see that her righteous son got the blessings. Rebekah used her influence to see that the priesthood blessings and keys passed to the righteous son. It's a perfect example of the man who has the keys and the woman who has the influence working together to ensure their blessings." (Beck, Julie B, "Teaching the Doctrine of the Family," *Ensign*, August 2009, pp. 71-74).

Blessings come from faithfulness, not favoritism or age (See Hebrews 11:20). The Lord inspires His servants to accomplish His will despite their weaknesses or incomplete knowledge of a situation. Isaac could have removed the blessing and bestowed a curse, but he did not (:12, and 33). You can't receive the blessings without obeying the commandments. It was Esau, not Isaac or Jacob, that lost the blessing (:36). Why do you think Esau tried to blame others for his mistakes? If we act like Esau in how we treat our sacred privileges, then we will have a moment of regret like Esau (:34-38).

Look for how Rebekah used her gifts as a mother to protect both the life of Jacob and the Abrahamic Covenant in verses 41-46. As a parent are you protecting your child's covenants as well as you do their lives?

Day 48, Genesis 28

In verses 1-5, Isaac blessed and counseled Jacob to marry in the covenant so that he might obtain the blessings of Abraham. Jacob was then sent to Rebekah's brother Laban to find a wife. Seeing that his choices disappointed his parents, Esau married one of the daughters of Ishmael. Though she is of the family, she is not of the covenant. This would be the modern-day equivalent of marrying someone who is less-active.

Verses 10-22 contain Jacob's sacred temple experience at Bethel. We know this is a temple experience because of the names used and ways that Jacob referred to the place in verses 17-19. In verse 12, Jacob saw a ladder that extended from the earth toward heaven. Joseph Smith taught that Jacob's vision of the ladder was a vision of the three degrees of glory (*Teachings*, 304-305). This was an old vision that was not understood until D&C 76. Elder Marion G. Romney taught that the rungs on the ladder represent the covenants that we make with God (*Ensign*, Mar 1971, 16). How many of these rungs can you label and name? Where are you on this ladder?

Look at the promises that God made with Jacob in verses 13-15. President David O. McKay said the following about the endowment: "Brothers and sisters, I believe there are few, even temple workers who comprehend the full meaning and power of the temple endowment. Seen for what it is, it is the step by step ascent into the eternal presence. If you young people could but glimpse it, it would be the most powerful spiritual motivation of your lives" (Truman G. Madsen. *Presidents of the Church* p. 269-270).

What does this quote and Jacob's vision help us understand about the importance of the temple covenants? These blessings are worth all the commandments and tithing that it takes to be worthy to enter the temples (:22).

Day 49, Genesis 29-30

As you read Genesis 29:1-30, look for what is poignant about this love story, and look for what is awkward about it. You may want to mark Genesis 29:20, and you may want to insert a scream in the appropriate location in Genesis 29:25.

Polygamy is a righteous principle when, and only when, its practice is commanded by God (D&C 132:37, and Jacob 2:28-30). Despite the fact that it was a commandment, plural marriage was hard on several that lived it. To discover God's reasons why He commanded plural marriage, search D&C 131-132 and Jacob 2:28-30. It is through plural marriage that we will see the creation of the twelve tribes of Israel. As you read Genesis 29:31-30:24, draw the family on a piece of paper and name and number the children as they come along. Using the footnotes to discover the meaning of the names is also interesting. When there are times that we feel alone and forgotten by God, we should remember Genesis 30:22.

Though we do not understand everything that was going on in Genesis 30:25-43, it is obvious that the Lord was fulfilling His promises to Jacob and blessing him.

Day 50, Genesis 31

What are the several reasons, given in verses 1-16, for why Jacob should leave after working for Laban for 20 years? Why is verse 16 the best advice ever?

As you read the account of Jacob fleeing, Laban tracking him down, and their confrontation in verses 17-42 look for how God helped and protected Jacob. The idols that Rachel stole are thought to also have a legal description of her property that was stolen by her father (:15). Still weird though, right?

In verses 43-54, Jacob and Laban built a heap out of rocks and covenanted that they will never pass by the heap to do the other harm (:52). With whom in your family do you need to build a heap?

In verse 55, Laban blessed his children and grandchildren. Even though fathers may be less-than-honorable in their priesthood service, they still have the right to give blessings to their family.

Day 51, Genesis 32

In verses 1-6, Jacob sent word ahead to let Esau know he was coming. Jacob then learned that Esau was coming with 400 men. This doesn't look good for Jacob. At first, Jacob divided his family into two camps, so that at least one would live (:7). Next, Jacob did what is the solution to all our problems: he approached God for help (:9-12). What problems and situations do you need to prayerfully take to God?

After seeking heaven's help and inspiration, Jacob divided his property up to present in groups of gifts to Esau to soften his heart (:13-22). Jacob didn't run away from the problem, but prayed for help did what he felt inspired to do and then continued to drive and move toward the problem in faith (:16). That night, Jacob had the family move ahead and he stayed alone to engage in personal prayer (:22-23). In verses 24-26, note how much Jacob wanted God to bless him. Why must we wrestle blessings from God; why doesn't He just give them up easily? When you have problems, how hard do you work at wrestling them for God? What wrestle does God want you to have with Him at this time?

Because of his faith to wrestle, look for what blessings, names, and meaning of names were given to Jacob in verses 26-30. What does this story teach you about what it means to be of the house of Israel?

Day 52, Genesis 33

We have all had fights with family members. Esau and Jacob's fight is now 20 years old. Look in verses 1-4 to see how this fight ends. What must have happened to Esau's heart over this time? How do you think this made Jacob feel? How can you act more like Esau and Jacob with your own family?

Look for evidences that Jacob and Esau had become humble and thankful men in verses 5-11. Both Esau and Jacob said the phrase, "I have enough" (:9, and 11). In what ways might this phrase be helpful in your life?

In verses 12-20, Jacob built a house and an altar.

Day 53, Genesis 34

Dinah is the only girl in a family with eleven brothers. What kind of life do you think she had? Do you think the story in verses 1-12 is a love story or a lust story?

In verses 13-31, you will read about plan of Dinah's brothers and the fulfillment of that plan. In what ways was the sin of Simeon and Levi worse than Shechem's?

What do you suppose we are to learn about lust and revenge from these sad stories?

Day 54, Genesis 35-36

This will be Jacob's third trip to Bethel. One trip to the temple is not enough, and it is best if you can get your family to go with you. Look in verses 1-4 for what the family does to get ready to attend the temple — the House of God, the Gate of Heaven. How do we make sure we are prepared to enter the temple? What "strange Gods," strange ideas, philosophies, and actions do the temple recommend questions make sure we have put away (:4)?

Verses 5-15 contain the family's temple experience and the renewal of the Abrahamic Covenant.

Every family has tragedies, and Jacob's is no exception. What was the tragedy in each of these sections: 16-19, 21-22, and 27-29? What can we learn from knowing that Jacob and his family, though righteous, had difficult and tragic things happened to them?

Genesis 36 contains a record of Esau's descendants.

Day 55, Genesis 37

In the last few chapters, we have seen reasons for why Reuben, Simeon, and Levi should not be given the birthright. In Genesis 38, we will learn why Judah was also not a suitable candidate. This is the third generation in a row that the blessing and birthright were bestowed because of righteousness and not age. As you read verses 1-11, look for the assorted reasons that Joseph's brothers did not like him. Do you think members of the Church sometimes act like young Joseph? How could we maintain better relationships with those who don't believe in dreams and visions, without dismissing what we have experienced?

How would you summarize verses 12-36 using the words "pit," "plot," "peer pressure," "problems," and "pain?"

One of the reasons Joseph will get so many pages dedicated to his story is because of the great symbolism between him and Christ. Identify the similarity between Joseph and Christ in verses 2, 3, 4, 7, 9, 13, 18, 22, 23, 24, 25, 26, 28, 31, and 34. Some may require a lot of thinking.

Day 56, Genesis 38

This chapter contains a heartbreaking story. What is a situation in which people may be tempted to lose virtue and chastity? As you read verses 1-12, you may find it helpful to draw a stick figure of each of the different people and put Xs on their eyes when they die. If the oldest son dies, and has no children with his wife, it is the duty of the next son to marry his brother's wife and have children with her so they might be able to take care of the widow. After the death of Onan, Judah was reluctant to give Shelah to marry Tamar because of his age.

When Judah did not provide Shelah as husband to Tamar, note what Tamar did to make sure Shelah is cared for in verses 13-30. How did Judah have different standards for men and women when it came to chastity? Judah did not think of the woman as someone's daughter, but merely a way to gratify his desires. In what ways does pornography cause us to only think of people as objects instead of sons and daughters, husbands and wives, and fathers and mothers? Real intimacy is to cause greater unity and love, not fracturing and objectification.

It is through this unlawful relationship that the line of Savior will be born.

Day 57, Genesis 39

God can help us to prosper in any circumstance. Look in verses 1-6 for evidence that this is true. What did you find?

Yesterday we saw how Judah lost his virtue and chastity through his choices. As you study verses 7-12, look for what helped Joseph to retain his virtue and chastity. What about this situation could have made it easy to give in? Every time we find ourselves in a situation where our virtue and chastity could be in danger, we must do as Joseph did when he "fled and got him out" (:12).

The false accusation of Potiphar's wife resulted in Joseph being cast into prison (:13-20). Do you still believe the principle at the beginning of today's entry? If that principle worked for a slave, will it also work for a prisoner? Look for evidence that it does in verses 21-23.

Day 58, Genesis 40

In verses 1-5, Pharaoh gets upset and imprisons both his butler and his baker, and both men have dreams that night. In verses 6-8, look for how

Joseph treated the men and their dreams. What do Joseph's actions teach us about how to treat others and how to understand dreams?

In verses 9-22, Joseph interprets the butler and baker's dreams. How do you think this knowledge helped each man? The butler promised to remember Joseph, but promptly forgot upon his release (:22). Who have you have forgotten to remember and thank for a recent kindness? It is not too late.

Elder Neal A. Maxwell said the following about Joseph:

> What a marvelous chance to take people to the length and breadth of family life and to see the maturation, the generosity, and the resilience. Of all the characters in scripture, except for the Savior, I know of none that have the resilience and the generosity of Joseph. Any one of the events which befell him would have been enough to ruin an ordinary person. He had been thrown into a pit and sold into slavery. Later in life he worked hard and was so trusted by his employer and his wife that when the wife falsely accused him, his employer did not support Joseph. He could have become bitter. He went to prison, ended up running the jail, and helped to get the butler out of jail. All he asked of the butler was that he remember him. The butler forgot him. There is still no recorded resentment. From that account, one can teach young people that bad breaks do not need to ruin a good man, or a good woman and that resilience can flow out of a generous spirit. ("The Old Testament: Relevancy within Antiquity" to S&I Aug 16, 1979, p.5)

Day 59, Genesis 41

How would you summarize verses 1-16 and then 17-32 if you were going to tell this story in your own words? Are you as quick to give God the credit as Joseph was in verse 16?

In verses 33-36, Joseph offered his advice after giving the interpretation. In what ways is Joseph's counsel still applicable for you in your circumstances?

Verses 37-57 covers Joseph's appointment, work, marriage, children, and fulfillment of Pharaoh's dreams.

Joseph's life was a constant pattern of ups and downs. Born eleventh. Became the favorite son. Thrown into a pit and sold as a slave. Became second in charge of Potiphar's house. Thrown into prison on false charges.

Becomes second in charge of the prison. Is forgotten after interpreting the butler's dream. Becomes second in charge of Egypt.

The names of Joseph's sons in verses 51-52 reflect the two lessons that he learned from this time in his life. Why are those two important lessons for everyone to learn and believe? When or how did Heavenly Father teach those lessons to you?

Day 60, Genesis 42

In what ways were the dreams and prophecies about Joseph from Genesis 37 fulfilled in Genesis 42:1-9?

An unrecognized Joseph challenged his brothers when they stated they were "true men" (:11, 19, 33, and 34). As you read verses 10-38, look for the different tests that Joseph created to see if his brethren still cared more for themselves than a single brother. What evidence do these verses give to suggest the brothers changed? In what ways is Joseph's testing of his brothers symbolic of the plan of salvation?

Notice in verse 21 how the brothers' guilt for what they did to Joseph had not dissipated. What vital steps of repentance were these brothers missing? Are there any past mistakes and sins for which you still feel guilty because you are missing vital parts in the process of real repentance?

Day 61, Genesis 43

With the food from their first visit to Egypt spent, and Simeon languishing in prison, Jacob was reluctant to send his sons back to Egypt with Benjamin. Note what the brothers did in verses 1-14 to convince Jacob to send Benjamin with them. In what ways is Judah's response in verses 8-9 a foreshadowing of the Savior, who will come through his descendants?

In verses 15-29, the brothers return to Egypt. Look for how they passed the tests that Joseph created to see if they are truthful and whether they have learned to control their love of money. How did they do? What evidence is there that they have changed? What do you love about Joseph's reaction to Benjamin in verse 30?

As the brothers sat down to eat in Joseph's house, what did he do in verses 31-34 that the brothers find amazing? Benjamin received more than the rest as a test to see if the brothers would become jealous if one brother was favored more than the rest, like he was.

Day 62, Genesis 44

In verses 1-17, look for Joseph's plan to get his brother Benjamin to stay with him, if the other brothers fail to prove they have changed.

Judah was the brother that originated the idea to sell Joseph as a slave because he couldn't see how killing him would profit them (Genesis 37:26). In verses 19-34 look for evidence that Judah was more concerned about others than he was about satisfying his own needs for his sexual appetite or financial gain.

In what ways does Judah's concern for his father and brother mirror the motivation of the Savior? How will you demonstrate this same motivation in your actions and interactions today?

Day 63, Genesis 45-46

Following Judah's plea to exchange places with Benjamin, Joseph revealed himself to the brothers. As you read Genesis 45:1-15, look for Joseph's perspective on how he views everything that has happened. What advice do you think Joseph would give to you and others during dark and discouraging days?

In what ways might the return trip have been difficult for the brothers, now that they have to be truthful and forthcoming about what really happened to Joseph years ago?

In Genesis 46, the family of Israel moved to Egypt. I love the tenderness of the embrace between the reunited Jacob and Joseph in verse 29. Do you think this is good foreshadowing of the embrace that will await you from your Heavenly Parents?

Day 64, Genesis 47

In verses 1-12, Joseph introduces Jacob and some of his brothers to Pharaoh, who allows them to shepherd in the choice land of Goshen.

My wife can attest that I love the topic of indentured servitude; she believes it is a conversation killer. Observe how the Egyptians became indentured servants to their government and lost their money, cattle, land, and themselves in verses 13-26. How could the financial principles of saving for the future and living within your means have helped to protect the people's freedom? How have these two principles helped you so far in your life? If you are not living these principles, will you begin to do so?

What does a dying Jacob make Joseph covenant to do in verses 27-31?

Day 65, Genesis 48

What does this chapter teach you about patriarchal blessings and the patriarchs that give them?

Verse 5 explains why Ephraim and Manasseh are included in the inheritance of the tribes of Israel. What do verses 16-19 teach us about the missions of these two tribes? Joseph's sons are to bless and save mankind even as Joseph blessed and saved his brothers.

Today would be a good day for you to study and ponder about your own patriarchal blessing. What blessings and promises are made in it? What warning and counsel are in it? What spiritual gifts are identified? Has your blessing become more significant over time?

Day 66, Genesis 49:1-27

The patriarchal blessings for the twelve tribes, or sons, of Israel are presented in this chapter (:28). Not all of the blessings were remarkable and wonderful because of the choices those sons made. How might some people's patriarchal blessings have been less powerful and hopeful if they were received later in life? As you read these blessings, try to make a few notes about each one. What do you think it means? Do you like it? What are the warnings, blessings or curses? The blessings of **Judah** and **Joseph** are important because of their significance and prophetic quality.

- Reuben's blessing is in verses 3-4.
- Simeon and Levi's blessings are in verses 5-7.
- **Judah's** blessing is in verses 8-12.
- Zebulun's blessing is in verse 13.
- Issachar's blessing is in verses 14-15.
- Dan's blessing is in verses 16-18.
- Gad's blessing is in verse 19.
- Asher's blessing is in verse 20.
- Naphtali's blessing is in verse 21.
- **Joseph's** blessing is in verses 22-26.

- Benjamin's blessing is in verse 27.

When are appropriate times in our lives for us to seek blessings from our fathers or other priesthood holders?

Day 67, Genesis 49:28-33 and Genesis 50:1-21

What do you love about how Genesis 49:29 and 33 refer to the death of Jacob? When have you felt that a loved one was "gathered home" when they died?

It is said that how a people care for the dead reveals their true level of love and commitment. Look at how Joseph cared for the body of his deceased father in Genesis 50:1-13. How have you shown your love and commitment to those who have died?

All parents know the nature of their children to get revenge when there are no parents around to enforce kindness. In Genesis 14-18, you will see the concern that Joseph's brothers experienced after their father's death. They were expecting a reckoning. Search Genesis 50:19-21 for phrases that create in you a desire to be better in all the relationships around you.

Day 68, Genesis 50:22-26 and JST Genesis 50:22-26 and JST Genesis 50:24-38

Genesis 50:22-26 finished the story of Joseph as his children make an oath to one day carry his bones to the land of his fathers. Footnote 24a takes us to JST Genesis 50:24-38, which contain over 40 different prophecies by Joseph of Egypt. As you read this inspired rendition, you may want to mark all the prophecies that you can find.

What did Joseph of Egypt prophecy about Moses, the Book of Mormon, and Joseph Smith Jr?

Day 69, Exodus 1

As you read verses 1-10, look for the circumstances that led to the children of Israel becoming the slaves of the Egyptians.

There were three different plans made to weaken and destroy the power of the people of Israel in verses 11-14, 15-21, and 22. Identify each plan and consider how well it worked. What can you learn about the potential success of the efforts of those who seek to destroy the Church or the people of God? What happened when the people were afflicted in verse 12? I love that, in verse 15, we get the names of these courageous women while the king's name is forgotten in the footnotes of history. How can you use the reasoning of these women in verse 17 in the situations you face?

Day 70, Exodus 2

How many tender mercies from God can you find in verses 1-10? What do you think Moses' mother's prayers and journal entry were like that night? If you were his mother and were granted this little extra time to be with and teach him, what would you make sure you taught him?

As you read verses 11-22 and D&C 84:6, which phrase do you think best describes this part of Moses' life: Moses loses everything or Moses gains everything? To better understand what is up with Moses killing a guy, check out Acts 7:22-29 and Hebrews 11:24-27.

In Exodus 1-2 we saw examples of God providing saviors for people. Look who still needed saving in verses 23-25.

Day 71, Exodus 3

Having reverence for sacred things is important for maintaining a sense of the sacred. Look for how both God and Moses showed reverence and respect for sacred things in verses 1-10. What are some things that have become sacred to you? What are things that the Lord would like you to treat more sacred?

Moses wanted to know how to introduce God to a group of people who had not known Him for some time. Look for how the Lord told Moses to introduce Him in verses 13-15. Why do you think God would want Himself introduced this way; what is He saying? What does the entry for "Jehovah" in the Bible Dictionary add to your understanding? If we add some extra words to this phrase, how many different things can you come up with?

- I Am full of…
- I Am going to…
- I Am never…
- I Am always…

Day 72, Exodus 4

Moses felt completely inadequate to lead the children of Israel out of Egypt. As you read verses 1-16, look for Moses' concerns and how the Lord resolves them. What do you think the Lord is trying to teach Moses and us from this? What reasons do you give yourself and others for why you can't be a great leader, teacher, parent, person, or miracle worker? How do you think the Lord would respond to those claims?

Moses was a great prophet. What do you think the Lord could have done with him if he didn't doubt himself so much?

In verses 24-27, Moses didn't circumcise his son and is almost killed by the Lord. Footnote 24a is helpful for a better understanding of this situation. In what ways does this appear to be a typical story of a wife and mother?

Day 73, Exodus 5

There are several things that people often must give up when they become members of the Church. This can be very difficult to change habits and cultures of a lifetime. Moses and Aaron were sent to ask Pharaoh and the people of Egypt to make some changes. Look for how Pharaoh responded to their invitation in verses 1-9. What are some of the important doctrinal details about God and His plan that people were missing (:2)?

Look for how life changed for the children of Israel in verses 10-21. If you were an Israelite, how would you feel about the efforts of Moses and Aaron? When God sends people to help change our lives, why doesn't it always get better at the beginning?

Look at how Moses felt about his calling and service in verses 22-23.

Day 74, Exodus 6

Moses was feeling very discouraged about his calling. I'm sure that you can probably relate to his struggles. Note the bold advice the Lord gave Moses in verses 1-8. You may want to mark the phrases "I have," "I am," and "I will." What was the Lord saying to Moses and to us when we feel our efforts are not helping?

Moses was finally feeling more confident, but the children of Israel rejected him again (:9). The Lord then asked Moses to again approach Pharaoh, but Moses was doubtful (:10-13). How do you save, lead, or teach people who don't want to be saved, led, or taught? The Lord's response is that you go, open your mouth, try, and He will provide the miracles (:9-13, and 26-30).

Day 75, Exodus 7

There are a couple of very helpful JST footnotes in this chapter (1b, 3a, 4a, and 13a). Not all of Joseph Smith's corrections to the text of the Bible were to restore original content or things that we lost. Some, like those in this chapter, were to clarify and increase readability. Clarifying past teachings is an incredible key role of prophets today as well. This is another reason why we need to be caught up on our General Conference reading.

In verses 1-14, what does the story about Moses, Aaron, and the sorcerers of Pharaoh changing their staffs into serpents teach you about each participant's authority?

Verses 15-25 contain the account of the first of 10 plagues upon Egypt. Notice that these miraculous events had an insignificant impact upon the heart of Pharaoh (13-14, 22-23, and 23a). Miracles don't soften people's hearts. Only the Spirit can do that.

Day 76, Exodus 8-9

Let's make a list of some of the plagues that fell upon Egypt. We traditionally call these the 10 plagues of Egypt, but I will propose that they were miracles to the children of Israel. As you read each of these, look for both the plague and the miracle in each event. I'll give you the verses, you write down the miracle. Note the point where the magicians of Pharaoh could no longer replicate the miracles.

- The second plague is in Exodus 8:1-15.
- The third is in Exodus 8:16-19.
- The fourth is in Exodus 8:20-32.
- The fifth is in Exodus 9:1-7.
- The sixth is in Exodus 9:8-11.
- The seventh is in Exodus 9:18-26.

Day 77, Exodus 10-11

Today we will continue to examine the 10 plagues or miracles that the Lord had Moses perform.

- The eighth plague is in Exodus 10:1-20.
- The ninth is in Exodus 10:21-29.
- The tenth is promised and foretold in Exodus 11:4-10.

Back in Exodus 7:5, the Lord said "the Egyptians shall know that I am the Lord." The Egyptians had a God that was to protect them from each of the 10 plagues. By the end of these plagues and miracles, how do you think the Egyptians felt about their Gods? How do you think they felt about the God of Israel? How do you think the children of Israel felt about their God? In what way has God proven to you that He is God above all others?

Day 78, Exodus 12

In verses 1-24, you will find instruction for the Passover, which is a sacred ordinance. Where can you see a shadow of the Savior in this ordinance?

Notice in verses 21-23 that it is not sufficient for there to have been a sacrifice, but that the blood had to be applied by the people who hoped for its protection, house by house. What can that action teach us about using the Atonement of Jesus Christ?

In verses 14, 17, and 24, the idea that the Passover is to happen "forever" is stated. So why don't we practice this ordinance today, or do we?

Notice how the Egyptians reacted to the destroying angel in verses 29-39.

Day 79, Exodus 13

In verses 1-16, the children of Israel are told to remember this day of deliverance when the Lord "by strength of hand brought us out of Egypt" (:3, 9, 14, and 16). We are to use the sacrament like the children of Israel were to use the Passover to teach the children (:14-16).

Like the children of Israel as they faithfully partook of the Passover, when we faithfully partake of the sacrament, we qualify to have the Lord lead us through the wildernesses of our lives as we seek to exist the world (:17-22).

Day 80, Exodus 14

Look at how Pharaoh and the Egyptians felt a few days after the children of Israel left in verses 1-9.

When the children of Israel saw the Egyptian chariots coming, note how they responded in verses 10-12. Why do you think they still didn't believe in Moses and the Lord?

In verses 13-14, look for lines that show Moses' faith. What is your favorite line? When things look dismal in your life, do you respond like the children of Israel or Moses?

The Lord's reply to this dismal circumstance is in verses 15-18. The Lord's people murmur, complain, and doubt. Yet, He still saves them and us. What miracles could He work if we responded with the faith of Moses?

Discover the ultimate results of all this in verses 19-31.

Day 81, Exodus 15

In verses 1-21, the children of Israel sang a hymn. Which of the following do you think best describes why they were singing: remembrance and memory, praise, thanksgiving and gratitude, testimony, or rejoicing? What are some of the reasons you sing hymns? Which modern hymn would you have sung if you would have been with Moses and the people?

Look for the problem they encountered three days after defeating the Egyptians in verse 22-24. What was the solution in verses 25-27? How can the tree be a symbol of Christ? The principle we learn from this story is that when bitter things encounter the Atonement, they become sweet. What bitter feelings or situations do you need Christ to heal and make sweet?

Day 82, Exodus 16

What did the children of Israel miss and murmur about in verses 1-3? Notice in verses 4-12 that the solution to hardships and misfortunes isn't to murmur about them, but to take the matter to God, as Moses does. Is there something that you need to stop murmuring about, and instead start praying about?

What spiritual lessons can we learn from the instruction on gathering manna in verses 14-31? How does asking us to do specific things consistently change our behavior and make us dependent upon God? What are the things that God asks you to repeat daily and weekly? What difference has daily seeking and gathering made in your life?

Look in verses 32-36 for how this bread became a powerful witness. What witnesses has God provided to you from your daily and weekly gathering of spiritual bread?

Day 83, Exodus 17:1-7

Look for similarities in verses 1-3 between how this chapter and the last both began. Temperatures in the wilderness of Sin can get as high as 120 degrees. Note what Moses did when he faced a problem in verse 4. Are you as quick to do what Moses did?

In what ways is the Lord's answer to Moses in verses 5-7 also an incredible object lesson about Jesus Christ? Why strike the rock? Why strike the rock before the water can come forth? Why do you think it was Moses that struck the rock?

Day 84, Exodus 17:8-16

Amalek brought an army to battle against the children of Israel (:8). Look for what the success of the battle depended upon in verses 9-11. How hard do you think Moses tried when he could see the other side destroying his people? What did Aaron and Hur do to assist in verses 12-16? In what ways is this a marvelous example of sustaining your leader? Can prophets and other church leaders do it all on their own? Which of the people mentioned in this story do you feel resembles you in your Church calling right now? When you sustain the prophet or your bishop, do you only do it with your hand, or is your heart in it as well?

Day 85, Exodus 18:1-27

In verses 1-12, Jethro brought Moses' wife and his two sons to be reunited. Moses recounted everything that had happened. What miracles and moments do you think Moses was excited to tell his two boys about? When was the last time you shared a miraculous moment with your family members?

Look what happened the next day in verse 13. What concerns did Jethro express about this practice in verses 14-18? What counsel did Jethro provide to Moses in verses 19-23? What great principles of leadership and gospel government did you learn from this experience? What do you think would have happened if Jethro hadn't spoken up? When have you received or provided the help necessary to keep a leader from wasting away?

Day 86, Exodus 19

Most people have a collection of some kind. In verses 1-6, look for what things the Lord treasures. What must these treasures do to meet the qualifications to become a collectable?

In verses 7-15, look for how the Lord wanted the people to prepare for what was essentially their temple experience. What must people do today to make sure they are worthy to enter the temple?

How does your first temple experience compare with what the children of Israel experienced in verses 16-25? Is this meant to be a frightening or exciting experience?

Day 87, Exodus 20:1-11

Yesterday we saw that the children of Israel were not quite ready to go to the temple and become a peculiar treasure of kings and queens. They had to become sanctified first. The purpose of the Ten Commandments is to show the standard of what a person must do to be worthy to go to the Mountain of the Lord, or the temple. Look for how the Ten Commandments are the foundation for a temple recommend.

Without looking, can you name the Ten Commandments in order? We will cover the four commandments that deal with our relationship with God today, in verses 1-11.

Satan has changed his tactic to get people to worship idols today. Instead of it being a religious thing, he has made it a cultural thing of habit, sport, recreation, and entertainment. How can you identify if something has become an idol?

What do you think is damaging about being casual when talking about God? Obviously it doesn't diminish His power.

Why do you think the commandment to observe the Sabbath day gets many more verses than any other commandment?

Day 88, Exodus 20:12-26

The first four commandments focus on our relationship with God. The next six commandments, in verses 12-17, speak to our relationship with other people. Thus, all the commandments really do rest on loving God and our fellow man (Matthew 22:35-40).

Have you personally witnessed the destruction of an individual or family from the failure to follow any of these commandments mentioned today?

If you changed the "Thou shalt not" commandments in verses 13-17 into commandments of "Thou shalt," what types of things is God expecting of us?

When the people saw the great witnesses of God's presence upon the mountain, they became frightened and backed away (:18-21). What kinds of things cause people to back away from their commitment to enter the temple and make covenants with God in our day?

Day 89, Exodus 21-22

"Sorry" isn't enough to be worthy of a temple recommend, according to Exodus 21:23-25. These are some of the most misunderstood verses in the scriptures. The Law of Moses is about restitution, not retaliation and revenge. Exodus 21-22 are examples of trying to get it right by making it right. Why does the Lord require that we make restitution as part of the repentance process? What does Exodus 22:31 add to your understanding about why we need to make restitution? As you read today's chapters, ponder on this question: Are there things that I need to do to make restitution for the things that I have done?

Day 90, Exodus 23

After keeping the Ten Commandments, repenting, and making restitution, the Lord also expects His people to follow the counsel in verses 1-9. There are several helpful footnotes to these verses that are still timely.

To help the people renew and remember their covenants, the Lord asked them to participate in rituals and feasts (:10-19). In which regular rituals does the Lord have you participate to help you to remember and renew your covenants?

As you read verses 20-33, look for the promises of divine help. What divine help have you benefited from this week?

Day 91, Exodus 24

What are some of the admission standards that colleges and universities have? Why do they have these? God has His own admission standards, but they are not based upon your GPA, ACT, or SAT score. Being admitted into the presence of God is based upon how well a person makes and keeps covenants (:3-8). Look for what blessings were bestowed upon this group of covenant-makers in verses 9-11. The covenants we make and keep to be admitted into the presence of God also change us so that we become more like God as we keep them. How have the covenants you have made so far changed you?

What happened to Moses in verses 12-18, and why might it have been disconcerting to the children of Israel?

Day 92, The Tabernacle, a Portable Temple

Israel's problem was not that they were stuck in Egypt, but that they had Egypt stuck in them—a predicament that mirrors our own. The antidote that was revealed to Moses was and is the temple. The temple is the means to escape the bondage of the world and then live in the presence of God. We, like the children of Israel, need an exodus (Exodus 25:8-9, 22).

Look up "Tabernacle" in the Bible Dictionary. Do a Google image search for "Tabernacle." Using the information and the images that you found, draw your own image of what the Tabernacle looked like below. Make sure you include each of the essential elements listed in tomorrow's section.

Day 93 Part 2, Exodus 25-27, and 30

Below you will find references to several of the most essential elements in the Tabernacle. As you read about each important piece of the Tabernacle, consider how that item might be used to teach about exiting the world, entering the presence of God, exiting Egypt, or the Fall of Adam and Eve.

- Exodus 25:10-25.
- Exodus 25:26-40.
- Exodus 26:1-18.
- Exodus 26:19-37.
- Exodus 27:1-21.
- Exodus 30:1-19.
- Exodus 30:20-38.

Day 94, Exodus 28

Years ago, I had a friend who felt very uncomfortable when he attended the temple for the first time. What made my friend uncomfortable was the temple clothing. He was not expecting these sacred vestments. If my friend would have studied Exodus 28, he would have learned that nearly all the temple clothes are mentioned (:2-4, 15, 37, and 42). The Church of Jesus Christ of Latter-day Saints made a wonderful video about the clothing in the temple. Google "LDS Sacred Temple Clothing Video," then watch it. What questions did that video answer? What questions do you still have? After you have watched the video, read Exodus 28 and see how much of the temple clothing is the same, even without the precious stones and metals.

In verse 36, you get a phrase that is engrave on most temples. Why? What do you think it means?

Day 95, Exodus 29

In verses 1-9, look for some of the things people can expect to happen when they go through the temple.

Verses 10-12 make sense when the symbolism is explained. Horns are a symbol of power. Blood is a symbol of the Atonement of Jesus Christ. The four corners—or directions of North, East, South, and West—are symbolic of the whole Earth, or every nation, kindred, tongue, and people. Thus, the message of these verses is: "There is power in the Blood of the Lamb for the whole earth."

The right side of the body is symbolic of a covenant, or that one is making a covenant. Try to figure out the symbolism in verses 19-21. Why the tip, thumb, and great toe?

With all the symbolism, there is a lot to ponder, but don't forget the main purposes of temples. Look in verses 42-46 to discover why tabernacles and temples are built.

Day 96, Exodus 31

Look for how the Lord used the talents and skills of a few choice individuals to bless many others in verses 1-11. What talents, skills, and gifts do you have to offer to the Lord? How has the Lord used your talents and gifts to bless the lives of others?

The Sabbath is both a sign from God to us and from us to Him (:13, 16-17). God has given us the Sabbath as a sign of how much He knows we need sanctification and as a sign of how much He wants to sanctify us. What sign does your behavior on the Sabbath send to God?

In verse 18 we learn that the commandments were written on stone. Why stone? God likes us to write down what He teaches us. How have you recorded the sacred communications that you have received from God?

Day 97, Exodus 32

Because Moses was gone for 40 days, look at what dumb choice the children of Israel made in verses 1-6. In verses 7-14, The Lord told Moses about what the people were doing. In these verses, it appears as though God was angry and Moses had to talk Him into repenting. The JST footnotes 12a and 14a help this make more sense.

In verses 15-35, Moses came down the mountain and destroyed the commandments and the golden calf. He then pounded the calf into a powder, which He made the people drink. Moses then asked, "Who is on the Lord's side?" (:26). With the sons of Levi by his side, Moses had them kill 3,000 unrepentant sinners. Why do you think the Israelites would stop their progression towards Jesus Christ and instead direct their attention and devotion towards a golden calf? What things are demanding your attention and devotion?

Day 98, Exodus 33

Which of the following do you think is the easiest to control: dogs, cats, donkeys, teenagers, adults, or the children of Israel? What word did the Lord use to describe Israel in verses 3-5? What does that word mean? Do you think this is a condition with which modern day Israel also struggles?

Because of their sins, the children of Israel lost the tabernacle and the opportunity to enter the Lord's presence. What great principles can you learn in verses 7-23 by reading about the interaction between the Lord and His prophet?

Verse 20 may seem to be at odds with verse 11 until you look at footnote 20a.

Day 99, Exodus 34

What does the Lord instruct Moses to do in verses 1-4? What did the Lord teach Moses about His attributes, character, and personality in verses 5-7? Because of what he learned about the Lord, Moses made a bold request of the Lord in verses 8-9.

In verses 10-27, the Lord said He would make a covenant to drive out the current inhabitants of the Promised Land—if the children of Israel don't go "a whoring after their gods" (:15-16). Several feasts and rituals were then established as a reminder of the covenant.

Moses remained with the Lord, fasting for 40 days. When Moses came down the mountain, his face shone because he was changed or transfigured while with the Lord. The people then had Moses veil his face (:28-35). Veils are meant to serve as reminders that the earthly are not always prepared to be in the presence of the divine. There is a separation between heaven and earth, but veils are also not meant to unmovable. Veils are meant to be thinned, removed, and uncovered in the proper place and time. To have one's face veiled is a spiritual compliment in anticipation of one day moving through the veil and into the presence of Him who will transfigure us.

Day 100, Exodus 34 Part 2

To understand everything that the incident with the golden calf cost the children of Israel, see the JST footnote 1a, D&C 84:17-27, and Mosiah 13:29-30. Building golden calves is foolish. They give us nothing and take away that which is of eternal value. Anything that keeps us from being worthy to go to the temple is a golden calf. What are some of the golden calves that are out there? Here are a few I would suggest:

- Breaking the Word of Wisdom.
- Failure to pay tithing.
- Not attending church meetings or serving in the Kingdom.
- A few gratifying moments of sexual pleasure or arousal.
- Not repenting because there is a stronger fear of man than God.
- Friends who do not help us to choose the right.
- Valuing entertainment and foolishness over work, education, and spiritual goals.
- Early dating and steady dating while in the teen years.
- A focus on our personal identity that causes us to lose our eternal identity.
- Media consumption that degrades our thoughts, language, and behavior.

Day 101, Exodus 35

The gifts and treasures that would eventually be used to construct the Tabernacle were to be offered "willingly" (:5, 21-22, and 29). As you read this chapter and those specific verses, notice how "willingly" offered gifts were used to create holiness. When God gives you commandments, do you respond willingly, somewhat willingly, or unwillingly? Make a list of which commandments and promptings that you are often engaging with. Then list next to each one if you are "willing," "somewhat willing," or "unwilling." Why do you think God asks us to "willingly" give up our offerings and keep the commandments?

Day 102, Exodus 36-38

The people were asked to willingly offer up their possessions to supply the needed materials for the Tabernacle's construction. Note how the people responded in Exodus 36:1-7. Why do you think people are so generous with their time, talents, and money when it comes to the construction of temples? No temple or church building is ever dedicated until it is paid for in full.

Throughout these chapters, you will read—and you may want to mark—the words "he made" and "he overlaid." Moses went into such detail about the constructing of the Tabernacle because this was the building in which he would perform sacred ordinances to become like God. He loved the temple. It is a man-made heaven, designed to get us to heaven. Think of the temples that you have visited. What parts of these temples do you find most beautiful? Think of the time, talents, and money that were sacrificed to produce these structures. What lesson is the temple teaching us about how to achieve heaven in its very construction?

Day 103, Exodus 39-40

You may want to find and mark the phrase "as the Lord commanded" in Exodus 39:5, 7, 21, 26, 29, 31, 32, 42, and 43, as well as in Exodus 40:16, 19, 211, 23, 25, 27, 29, and 32. Everything about the temple and its construction is evidence that we have a people who will follow the commandments of God. How does the temple help you keep the commandments of God?

It is only after the people were obedient in keeping the commandments that they received a pillar of fire and a cloud of smoke to guide them (Exodus 40:34-38). If we want divine guidance, then we must obey the commandments. Look up the word "Shechinah" in the Bible Dictionary and see what more you can learn about this pillar of fire, or cloud of smoke.

Day 104, Leviticus 1

The book of Leviticus is a handbook for priests on how to perform animal sacrifices, so there is a lot of cut-up animals, blood, burning, and ashes. The book of Leviticus also uses the word "Atonement" more than any other book in scripture. That little piece of knowledge will change the way that you read about these sacrifices because every offering, priest, animal, and sacrifice is a symbolic representation of Jesus Christ and His offering. Let's do one: As you study Leviticus 1:1-13, look for as many symbols of Christ as you can find, then look again.

Day 105, Leviticus 2-7

The other offerings in Leviticus 2-7 have similar symbolism as the burnt offering that we learned about yesterday. If you want to study more about these other ordinances, look up "sacrifice" in the Bible Dictionary.

If we are doing it right, the sacrament can be a spiritually rejuvenating experience. What do you think the participants in these animal sacrifices felt as they pondered upon the symbols? In what ways do you think the ancient saints might be shocked by the symbolism of the sacrament?

Day 106, Leviticus 8-10

In chapter 8, Aaron and his sons went through a beautifully symbolic ordinance. In verse 23, blood was placed upon the tip of their right ears, thumbs, and great toes. The ear, hand, and foot represent our ability to listen, obey, and act. Having blood placed upon the tips of these appendages is to show greater diligence and adherence. It shows us how Christ listened, obeyed, and acted. Aaron and his sons covenanted to do the same. How well have you listened, obeyed, and acted like Jesus Christ this week?

Proper performance and participation in priesthood ordinances prepares us to see and feel the glory of the Lord. The Lord's power is manifested in two remarkable ways in Leviticus 9:23-24, and 10:1-2. Why do you think these offerings produced such drastic results?

What does Leviticus 10:8-11 teach you about the propose of the priesthood?

Day 107, Leviticus 11

This chapter contains the law of kosher. *Kosher* in Hebrew means fit or proper. Verses 1-43 contains the dietary rules for what the children of Israel could and could not eat. Look for the purpose of this law in verses 44-47. If they had to determine what was clean and unclean every time they ate food, then maybe they would also start to do that with their thoughts and actions. As you go through the day, ponder on how often you are presented with a choice between clean and unclean things. How can this help you to be more holy, like our God (:44)?

Day 108, Leviticus 12-15

Leviticus chapter 12 lists the amount of time a woman must wait for purification following childbirth.

Because of its corruptive and contagious qualities, the disease of leprosy is frequently used as a symbol for sin. Read in this light, Leviticus 13-14 can be very instructive for how a church leader should minister to a person who is struggling to overcome sin. What did you learn from these chapters about how to help or be helped?

Speaking about Leviticus 15:1-7, Elder Russel M. Nelson said,

It was only a short century ago that the great work of Koch, Pasteur, and others proved that infection could be caused by bacteria in contaminated body fluids—or infected issues—passed from one individual to another. With these highlights of history in mind, may I quote the word of the Lord recorded long ago in Leviticus, chapter fifteen: . . . Thus, our loving Heavenly Father had clearly revealed principles of clean technique in the handling of infected patients more than three thousand years ago! These scriptures are in complete harmony with modern medical guidelines. But during those many millennia, how many mothers needlessly perished? How many children suffered because man's quest for knowledge had failed to incorporate the word of the Lord? ("Where Is Wisdom?" Ensign, Nov 1992, 7).

Day 109, Leviticus 16-17

Leviticus 16 covers the most holy day of the Jewish fasts, Yom Kippur, or the Day of Atonement. To better understand this sacred day, look up "Fasts" in the Bible Dictionary and read the 2-3 paragraphs.

The two goats are both symbols for Christ. I think that we understand the symbol of the goat in verses 15-16 better than we do the goat in verses 20-22. What do you think? What have you learned in your life about how to place your hands on the Atonement and let Jesus take away sins, guilt, and all other unpleasantness? How much do you think the Savior desired to take these types of things away from us? Are you holding on to a struggle, guilt, or discouragement that you will not allow the Savior to take into the wilderness for you?

Day 110, Leviticus 18 and 20

Look for what the Lord told the children of Israel that He didn't want them doing and for what He wanted them to be in Leviticus 18:1-3, 24-30; and Leviticus 20:7-8, 22-23, 26.

What were the other currently inhabited nations doing, according to Leviticus 18:6-23 and Leviticus 20:1-6, 9-21? After reading about these nations, can you understand why the Lord asked the Israelites to destroy these people? In what ways is the Lord's justice upon the wicked a sign of His mercy to the righteous?

Day 111, Leviticus 19

Israel was about to live in the middle of a corrupt group of people. How were they supposed to be able to do this, according to verse 2? Why is this such a great principle for those who find themselves surrounded by wickedness?

Search verses 3-4, 9-20, and 28-37 for how the children of Israel are supposed to be different so they can make a difference.

How many ways can you finish this statement: "The Lord wants you to be holy like Him by doing…"

Day 112, Leviticus 21-23

As you read in Leviticus 21 about the physical requirements and blemishes that would disqualify a man from serving as a priest, consider modern standards. What does it teach us about Christ to have those who symbolize Him not have the things listed in verses 17-20?

In Leviticus 22, the priests are promised that they and their families will be provided for from the sacrifices of the children of Israel.

Look up "Feast" in the Bible Dictionary to learn more about each of these special occasions and how they are designed to direct the participant to greater devotion.

- Leviticus 23:1-3 speaks of the Sabbath day.
- Leviticus 23:4-14 is about the Feast of Unleavened Bread, or Passover.
- Leviticus 23:15-23 explains the Feast of Weeks, or Pentecost.
- Leviticus 23:26-32 outlines the Day of Atonement, or Yom Kippur.
- Leviticus 23:33-44 describes the Feast of Tabernacles.

Day 113, Leviticus 24-25

What do you think is the symbolic purpose of the perpetual light, incense, and shewbread mentioned in Leviticus 24:1-9?

Leviticus 24:10-23 lists several offences that would result in capital punishment. The principle behind this type of punishment was explained in Exodus 21-22 on Day 89.

Leviticus 25 so impressed Elder L. Tom Perry that he twice spoke about the idea of Jubilee in General Conference ("A Meaningful Celebration," Oct 1987; "A Year of Jubilee," Oct 1999). Look up either talk to gain some insights about this remarkable chapter and the celebration it outlines.

Day 114, Leviticus 26-27

What promises does the Lord make to those who keep the commandments in Leviticus26:1-13?

What are the promises if we break the commandments in Leviticus 26:14-39?

What are the promises if we repent and return in Leviticus 26.40-46?

Look in Leviticus 27:30-33 to discover how the Lord feels about tithing.

Day 115, Numbers 1-4

In Numbers 1, the males who could participate in battle are numbered. In Numbers 2, we learn the layout of the camp of Israel. The tabernacle was pitched in the middle with three tribes on each side to surround the camp. This organization of the camp also helps explain the purpose of organized religion. The Lord has always organized His camp and Church to provide protection and direction to the temple. If a person chooses not to participate in the organization of the Church, then there will be less protection and direction to the temple in their life. What protections and directions to the temple have you received in your life by participating in the organization of the Church?

In Numbers 3:24, 28, 31, and 38, we see that every member has a "charge" to accomplish. Then, in Numbers 4, we see that every member has a responsibility to help move the Church along. What charges and callings have you had that have helped to move the Church along? How does your charge to move the Church help provide protection and direction to others?

Day 116, Numbers 5-6

What are the simple and profound gospel principles that can be found in Numbers 5, which describes some interesting practices?

Missionaries of the ages of 18 and 19 years have made vows that makes them different from others of similar age. What are some of the things missionaries can and can't do when compared to their contemporaries? The Nazarites in ancient Israel made similar vows. Mark all variations of the word "separate" in Numbers 6:1-8 and 18-21. What are some of the things the Nazarites vowed to do to be separate?

What do we do, or what can we do, to separate ourselves from the world? Have you sufficiently separated yourself from the world so that God knows that you are on His team?

Look in Numbers 6:24-27 to discover the promised blessings for separating ourselves.

Day 117, Numbers 7-10

Numbers 7 contains the calling and sacrifices of the 12 princes or apostles. Find and mark their names. Verse 89 is also worth marking. Read the chapter heading for Numbers 8.

In addition to the tabernacle and the surrounding tribes camped around it, what additional image needs to be included to complete the camp of Israel in Numbers 9:15-16? What else can you learn about this pillar of fire, or cloud of glory, from Numbers 9:17-23? How can these lessons make us better followers of God? Where will God have you journey today? Will you follow the nudges of the cloud and pillar?

Look for any other ideas that teach you about how to journey through life as you study Numbers 10.

Day 118, Numbers 11

What should we learn about complaining from verses 1-3? Even after the earlier mentioned punishment, there is more complaining. Look for who was complaining and what their complaints were in verses 4-10 and 11-15. Do you sympathize with the complaints of ether group?

The Lord provided solutions to both complaints. To Moses' grief, the Lord offered a solution in verses 16-17 and 24-30. What principle did you learn about how the Lord seeks to help the leaders of His Church? Are you a person who helps to alleviate the grief of Church leaders, or do you supply it?

The Lord's solution to the complaints offered by the Children of Israel, in verses 18-23, and 31-34, may seem harsh. From this punishment, we learn that God—who is all-powerful, all-knowing, and all-merciful—will never be enough for those who are unthankful, forgetful, and lustful. Does is story increase your desire to complain less and be more thankful to God?

Day 119, Numbers 12

What fault did Aaron and Miriam find with Moses in verses 1-3? How did this discovery make Aaron and Miriam feel about themselves? Why do you think people often put others down to feel better about themselves? It is important to know that Moses was commanded to do this thing (D&C 132:1, and 38).

What did the Lord say and do in verses 4-10 to those who were critical of His prophet? How is this punishment a great symbol and warning for those who criticize the prophet today?

How does Moses' response in verses 11-16 prove what verse 3 said? When people are critical of you and get what they deserve, do you respond as well as Moses?

Day 120, Numbers 13-14:3

In Numbers 13:1-25, 12 spies were selected and sent into the Land of Canaan to discover the strength of the current inhabitants.

Every situation is an opportunity to demonstrate our faith or doubts. As you read Numbers 13:26-33, look for the voices of doubt and voice of faith. What reasons were given by those who doubted? Do you typically face demanding situations with a voice of doubt or faith? How will you face an expected challenge with greater faith today? How will you remember to act in faith when an unexpected challenge arises?

To what voice did the Children of Israel chose to listen in Numbers 14:1-4? To where were they willing to return rather than face a demanding situation?

Day 121, Numbers 14:5-45

Yesterday we learned about the importance of facing problems with faith. How well did you do yesterday in your own life? Did you respond like Joshua and Caleb in verses 5-9? What did they believe that allowed them to act in faith?

Because of their faithless doubt, what consequences did God promise upon the Children of Israel in verses 10-38? Then, look for what was promised to Caleb in verse 24. If we can't face the mortal challenges of day-to-day living with faith, how can God ever lead us into the eternal Promised Land of the Celestial Kingdom? What fears, and doubts will you overcome with faith today? Go ahead believe and act like Caleb and Joshua.

Upon hearing the pronounced punishments, the people tried to change their minds, not because of faith, but from a fear of God. Look what happened from delaying the right action and acting on fear and doubt rather than faith in verses 39-45.

Day 122, Numbers 15-16

What can you learn from Numbers 15:22-36 about how the Lord holds people accountable at various levels depending upon membership and ignorance? How can this demonstrate God's ability to judge with mercy and justice? To continually remind the Children of Israel of His justice and mercy, God had them sew a blue ribbon into the hems of their robes, so that each step would be a reminder to walk within the bounds that had been set (Numbers 15:38-41).

Numbers 16 is a chapter of separation, in which God "will shew who are his, and who is holy" (:5). Korah and his crew came "against" Moses and Aaron with their complaints in verse 1-3. What kind of men made up this band, and what was their complaint?

As you read Numbers 16:4-50, watch for how the crew of Korah continued to separate themselves from God and His prophets by coming "against" them (:3, 11, 19, and 41-42). Can you see the same dangerous attitudes in some murmuring members today? In what modern ways do those who come against the Lord's prophets lose power and protection?

Day 123, Numbers 17-19

Because of the deaths of so many, some in the camp of Israel were questioning the leadership of Moses and Aaron. Look for what test the Lord designed to prove that Moses and Aaron have His authority in Numbers 17. What does this symbolic result teach you to expect when the Lord calls you to act in His name?

As you read in Numbers 18 about the charge to the Levites to administer the ordinances of the Tabernacle, note what they had to give up regarding their inheritance. What types of things do members of the Church give up so they can faithfully serve in the charge the Lord gives them? The Lord took care of the Levites with some of the tithing of the people (Numbers 18:23-28). What rewards and blessings have come to you for faithfully serving in your current charge?

The sacrifice of a red heifer in Numbers 19 was for the purification of those who have encountered a corpse. The symbolism, however, resembles the pattern a person would undergo when seeking to recover from spiritual death following an encounter with sin.

Day 124, Numbers 20

The incident at the beginning of this chapter will cost Moses and Aaron the right to lead the Children of Israel into the Promise Land. The Lord desires perfect obedience, and we miss out on blessings when we do not act according to His direction. As you read verses 1-5, look for reasons why Moses and Aaron might have been less patient with the Children of Israel than normal. What does verse 8 say that Moses was supposed to do? What did Moses and Aaron do instead in verses 9-11?

According to verse 12 and footnote 12a, how did Moses and Aaron fail to magnify the Lord before the people? This momentary mistake didn't cost them anything eternal, but they did lose out on present happiness. If Moses and Aaron failed to do what they were supposed to do, why do you think the Lord still brought forth water from the rock? Has the Lord ever magnified you, even when you have failed to magnify Him?

In verses 14-22, Edom, the descendants of Esau, refused to let the Children of Israel pass through their land. How much happiness is lost in your family because of sibling rivalry and unkindness?

Moses will lose both of his siblings by the end of this chapter. What great lessons can be learned from the funeral of Aaron in verses 23-29?

Day 125, Numbers 21

If you were the Lord, how would you be feeling about the Children of Israel after verses 1-5? Because of this repeated behavior, the Lord caused the events in verses 6-9. What lessons and symbolism can you discover about this story by using footnote 9a, John 3:14-21, and Helaman 3:13-16?

The task they had to accomplish to receive help was so easy, and yet they didn't do it. Are you daily using the help offered by the Lord through His Atonement, or are you hurting yourself by refusing to turn to Him?

Day 126, Numbers 22

After the destruction of the Amorites in the last chapter, Balak, the king of Moab, was concerned. In an attempt to curse the children of Israel, Balak sought to hire the prophet Balaam and use his priesthood to curse Israel. What did Balak do to entice Balaam in verses 1-20, and what did the Lord say about the situation? An enticing situation is one in which we are offered something to get us to oppose God's will. Will you look for and identify those situations today?

Verses 20-41 contain the story of a smart ass and a dumb prophet. Go ahead look for both as you read. Why do you think it was harder for the Lord to open the eyes of Balaam than it was the mouth of the donkey (:28-31)? How many times does God have to tell you something? Does God have to speak by the voice of an angel—or a donkey—or can He get your attention with the whispering of the Holy Ghost?

Day 127, Numbers 23-24

Three times Balak tried to get Balaam to curse Israel. They even tried different mountains, just in case God is more inclined to a particular place. As you read these three accounts, look for the blessing, rather than the curse, and for the great exchanges that followed between Balak and Balaam. Does the world ever make similar remarks as Balak? What do you love about how Balaam acts in these chapters?

- Numbers 23:1-12
- Numbers 23:13-26

- Numbers 23:27-24:25

Numbers 24:17-19 also contains a sweet prophecy by Balaam about Jesus Christ. Why do you think a star and a scepter are good symbols for Christ?

Day 128, Numbers 25-26

As we saw in Numbers 23-24, Israel could not be cursed if they were worthy. So, the Moabites used their women and their fertility worship of Baal to corrupt the men of Israel in Numbers 25:1-3. In what ways is Israel losing its power and blessings today because of sinful corruption? Notice that Phinehas attacked the problem in order to stop it in the rest of Numbers 25.

Numbers 26 contains the second numbering of army-aged men. In verse 64 look for which men didn't make the cut. All people of the earth will eventually be numbered. Will you be numbered among the following groups: full tithe-payer, active Church member, temple recommend holder, sealed, or clean? What other important numberings could you add to the list?

Day 129, Numbers 27-29

In Numbers 27:1-12, we learn that gender does not determine inheritance.

What great lessons about leadership and succession are taught in Numbers 27:13-23?

In the chapter headings of Numbers 28-29, you will see specified times for worship. Why do you think it is important to have practices of worship daily, weekly, and on holidays?

Day 130, Numbers 30-31

What important principle is taught in Numbers 30:2? This is always the rule, unless it is one of the three situations described in the rest of chapter 30.

In Numbers 31 the Lord had Moses make war against the Midianites for the corruption they caused in Numbers 25. All the adult males were killed. Among the dead was Balaam the prophet (:8). When He was not allowed to curse the children of Israel to collect his fee, Balaam then counseled the

Midianites on how to corrupt Israel with sexual sin so they would no longer be worthy (:16). What do you think is the final lesson that we are to learn from Balaam?

Because of the corrupting influence the Midianite women had on Israel, Moses was displeased when they were not destroyed with the men (Numbers 31:9-16). In verses 17-18, Moses had all Midianites who were corrupted by the sexual fertility worship of Baal-Peor destroyed. On occasion, God destroys people who have lost the ability to use their agency freely because of the completely corrupting influence of the tradition of their parents. How can this action, though harsh, be a protection for both the children of Israel and those destroyed?

Day 131, Numbers 32-33

In Numbers 32, the tribes of Reuben, Gad, and half of Manasseh wanted to receive their inheritance in the lands that Israel had already conquered, rather than in the conquered Promised Land of Canaan (:1-5). Moses was worried that if they stayed in the current land, the rest of the children of Israel would be dissuaded from entering the Promised Land (:6-15). In the rest of the chapter, these tribes promised that they would fulfill their obligation to serve and fight with the other tribes so that they would have a place of inheritance (:16-42). What lessons can this chapter teach to future potential missionaries, parents, and Church leaders?

Numbers 33 documents the journey to the Promised Land. You may want to mark the words "pitched," "removed," and "departed" in verses 3-49. What can the pattern of these words teach you about your journey to the Promised Land? In verses 50-54, the instruction for possessing the land of Canaan is given. Note the punishment for incomplete obedience or repentance in verses 55-56.

Day 132, Numbers 34-36

Rather than reading Numbers 34, find the map that shows the division of the twelve tribes in whatever edition of the scriptures you are using. Manasseh had two lands of inheritance because of Numbers 32. Why do you think there were such discrepancies in the size of the inheritances? How is this a good lesson about God's views on equality?

Look at your map again and locate the land that the tribe of Levi inherited. Numbers 35 will explain what you discovered. What does this explain about purpose priesthood? You may want to mark the phrase "cities of refuge" in verses 6, 11-12, 15, 25-28, and 32.

Why is the counsel in Numbers 36 no longer applicable? What words in the chapter heading would you have to change to make this counsel applicable?

Day 133, Deuteronomy 1-4

Deuteronomy means "repetition of the law" (Bible Dictionary). Chapters 1-3 recount the journey of the children of Israel from the time they left Mount Sinai or Horeb and traveled in the wilderness for 40 years.

The children of Israel were preparing to enter the Promised Land for 40 years. In Deuteronomy 4, Moses began to instruct the people on how they could be "a people of inheritance" (:20). As you read this chapter, look for what you need to do to make sure that you are worthy of an eternal inheritance in the true Promised Land.

Day 134, Deuteronomy 5-6

Deuteronomy 5 contains a second rendering of the Ten Commandments. As you read, look for additional understanding and clarity to come about these essential teachings. The first time the Ten Commandments were given was to prepare the children of Israel to meet their God on Mount Sinai. This rendition was given to prepare the wandering children of Israel for their entry into the Promised Land. For what do you think the Ten Commandments are preparing you?

The commandment and teaching from Deuteronomy 6:3-7 are so important that these words were written on small scrolls, beginning the practices of touching Mezuzahs and binding phylacteries to arms and forearms. These sacred practices continue among devout Jews even today (Deuteronomy 6:8-9, 8b, and 9a). They are designed to help the people remember the Lord (Deuteronomy 6:12). What are you doing to make sure that you and your family are consistently remembering the instruction of Deuteronomy 6:3-7?

Deuteronomy 6:14-25 is another great summary about why God has given us commandments.

Day 135, Deuteronomy 7-8

In Deuteronomy 7:1-3, the children of Israel were directed to harshly treat the people whom they will drive out of the Promised Land. It is important to remember the description of these people from Leviticus 18 and 20. What additional reasons did God give for wiping these people out in Deuteronomy 7:4-10? According to Deuteronomy 7:3-4, what are some of the reasons God is interested in whom His people marry?

For 40 years, the children of Israel wandered in the wilderness. As you study Deuteronomy 8, be on the lookout for the major lessons God was trying to teach to His people. Some of these lessons are mentioned in verses 2-3. What experiences has God given to you to teach the same lessons He was teaching ancient Israel?

Day 136, Deuteronomy 9-10

In Deuteronomy 9:1-6, an explanation was given for why Israel could inherit the Promised Land when other nations were currently living there. In what ways has your life been impacted by the righteous or wicked lives of others? The rest of the chapter is a rendering of the stiffneckedness of Israel. Why do you think Moses reminded Israel of their own sins when they started to think they were better than these other nations?

The Ark of the Covenant is a symbol of God's throne and presence. What do you think is the significance of the tables of stone containing the commandments that were placed inside the Ark? What about the Levites' opportunity to carry the Ark, but not receive an inheritance in the Promised Land (Deuteronomy 10:1-9)? The Israelites were to drive out other nations from the Promised Land because of their wickedness. Look in Deuteronomy 10:12-22 for the requirements to stay worthy of the Promised Land.

Day 137, Deuteronomy 11-13

The young children who were about to enter the Promised Land did not get to see the great miracles that were performed in Egypt. Therefore, it was essential for their parents to teach them. Read Deuteronomy 11:19-20 for God's instruction to parents about instructing their children. How did your parents do at this? How are you doing at this? What actions could you take to do this better?

Deuteronomy 12 can be summarized as a warning about places and environment. Deuteronomy 13 is a warning for Israel to beware of those who would have them participate in wrong doing.

Day 138, Deuteronomy 14-16

Since most of Deuteronomy is a repeat of what we have read earlier, I thought I would just give you a couple of highlights to examine today. Look up each of the scripture sections and try to identify a truth for each one. Then, write it down as clearly as you can.

- 14:1-2
- 14:22-23, and 38
- 15:1-2, 1b, 4-7, and 4a
- 15:9-11
- 16:16-17

Day 139, Deuteronomy 17-19

What counsel does Deuteronomy 17:8-14 have for dealing with very difficult matters to judge?

What is a king supposed to do and what is a king not supposed to do according to Deuteronomy 17:15-20?

In Deuteronomy 18:9-15, look for all the things other did instead of following a prophet.

What did Moses say about Jesus Christ in Deuteronomy 18:18-19?

How does Deuteronomy 18:21-22 say to discern a true prophet from a false one?

Day 140, Deuteronomy 20-23

When facing challenges, it is good to remember the advice in Deuteronomy 20:1-4. How helpful could it be to approach relationships the same way Israel was encouraged to approach their enemies in Deuteronomy 20:10-12?

Deuteronomy 21 is about laws to help care for people who are sometimes treated like they don't matter. Who is an unnoticed person for whom the Lord would have you show greater care?

How would you reword the commandment in Deuteronomy 22:1-4 to make it modern? Deuteronomy 22:13-30 show how serious chastity and sexual sins were considered.

Deuteronomy 23 lists several people who were not to be allowed in the camp and congregation of the Lord, and verse 16 explains why.

Day 141, Deuteronomy 24-26

Which laws in Deuteronomy 24-25 seem reasonable, and which ones seem strange?

When have you experienced the principles in Deuteronomy 26:6-9?

What does Deuteronomy 26:11 teach you about what you need to rejoice over?

Find out what the word "avouched" means. Then, study Deuteronomy 26:15-19 for what you can do to avouch the Lord and be avouched by Him.

Day 142, Deuteronomy 27-30

Find a bible map that shows both Gerizim and Ebol mountains. What did Moses have the children of Israel do with these two mountains in Deuteronomy 27:11-13?

What types of behaviors will bring about curses, according to Deuteronomy 27:15-26? If we diligently hearken to the voice of the Lord, Deuteronomy 28:1-14 mentions some of the blessings that we can expect. Look in Deuteronomy 28:15-68 for an extensive list of curses that can be expected for wickedness.

Deuteronomy has clearly established that making covenants with the Lord will result in tremendous blessings or curses (Deuteronomy 29).

Moses promised that Israel would experience each of the promised blessings and curses. As you read Deuteronomy 30, it will become very clear that we each get to decide if we will turn to the promised blessings or curses of the Lord.

Day 143, Deuteronomy 31-34

What advice did Moses give to all of Israel and Joshua in Deuteronomy 31:1-8, just before he left them?

One of the last things that Moses did to instruct the children of Israel was to teach them a song. Look in Deuteronomy 31:16-22 for the purpose of teaching this song. Do you believe songs about sacred things can really do that? Which hymns fortify you? The words of the hymns are wonderful. The song that Moses taught is no exception and it can be found in Deuteronomy 32:1-43.

Apostles sometimes leave apostolic blessings on groups of people. This is following the pattern presented by Moses as he blessed each tribe in Deuteronomy 33. Verses 16-17 also explain some of the symbolism of the oxen used in the temple.

In Deuteronomy 34, it is important to make sure you understand verses 6, 9, 10, and the footnotes that accompany them.

Day 144, Joshua 1

Moses was a prophet for over 40 years. What made Moses such a great prophet? What might have been some of the thoughts of Joshua, who was called to replace him? We have all experienced these fears and worries. Look for what the Lord said that might have provided comfort to Joshua at this time in verses 5-9. There is something in every verse.

Verse 8 alone should motivate us to have daily scripture study.

What are some things we are asked to do in the Church that are not convenient? The tribes of Reuben, Gad, and half of Manasseh lived east of the Jordan. They already had their land and were comfortable. Joshua asked if they would help the other tribes or if they were just going to stay comfortable. Their response is found in verses (:16-18). Will we be like these "mighty men of valour" in our service and commitments (:14)?

Day 145, Joshua 2

Joshua sent two men to spy out the land. For cover they went to the house of a harlot. When the king of Jericho learned of the spies he sought to find them. There was a danger that a woman who sold her body would be likely to sell out these two men (:1-3). Instead of betraying them, look for the help and testimony she offered in verses 4-11.

In exchange for helping the spies, look for what she requested in verses 12-15. Then, in verses 17-21, she was told what she must do to receive that which she had asked. What can these actions required of her symbolize about the Atonement?

What happened to this woman's life in one day? What was she? What did she become?

Day 146, Joshua 3

As the children of Israel finally prepared to enter the Promised Land, they ran into a challenging obstacle: The Jordon River was flooding and impossible to cross (:15). Read the whole chapter, and look for what this story teaches you about overcoming challenges and obstacles.

Why do you think they needed to be sanctified? (:5) Why do you think the Ark had to go first (:13)? Why do you think they needed to get their feet wet before the water parted (:13-16)?

When we have faith, it will lead us toward obstacles and challenges, knowing that as we get our feet wet, miraculous help will come. What obstacles and challenges do you need to move toward with faith?

Day 147, Joshua 4

While crossing the Jordan River, the Lord had Joshua select 12 men to gather 12 stones (:1-5). In verses 6-9 and 20-24, we discover the Lord had them do this to help the people remember. What do you think the difference might be between having people show the rocks rather than just telling the story?

Why do you think it is important to remember and record the miracles we have experienced? What miracles do you need to record that you have not?

In the last chapter, we learned that faith points us toward our challenges so we can experience miracles. In this chapter, we learn that faith is also built as we look back and remember how the Lord has helped us. Then, our faith will be prepared to face the next obstacle that is placed in our path toward eternal life.

Day 148, Joshua 5

In verses 1-8, the children of Israel were asked to perform a second circumcision. As you read these verses, consider why it is important that the covenants and sins of the parents are not automatically passed on to their children.

The miracle of the manna stopped in verses 9-12. Let's do some math with this miracle. For 40 years, the children of Israel gathered manna daily, except for on the Sabbath. That means this miracle was witnessed 12,520 times. Wow! What does this frequency say about God's willingness to provide help and miracles?

After entering the Promised Land, the next step was to conquer the other nations who were living there. Look for who showed up to help in verses 13-15. Some other helpful references are Revelations 19:19, 22:8-9, and Exodus 3:15.

Day 149, Joshua 6

As you read the battle plans for taking the city Jericho, why might it have been tempting for a member of the camp of Israel to doubt the plan and criticize it?

It wasn't silent marching, trumpets, or shouting that brought down the walls. What do you think was the real reason that this campaign was successful? In what ways can you use that same principal in your life today?

Day 150, Joshua 7-8

As you read Joshua 7, which of the following principles most impressed itself upon you?

- There is no such thing as private sin; all sin has consequences and will affect other people.
- It is impossible to hide wickedness from the Lord and His servants forever.
- I, like Israel, cannot progress until I confess and forsake my sins.

After their loss to the city of Ai in Joshua 7, look for how the children of Israel defeated them in Joshua 8.

Day 151, Joshua 9-11

In Joshua 9, the children of Israel made a foolish oath with the Gibeonites when they dressed up like vagabonds. Look for one of the reasons they made a mistake in Joshua 9:14. About which choices might you need to counsel with the Lord?

Because of Israel's oath with Gibeon, five cities came to battle against them. Look for the details of this battle in Joshua 10:7-27. What did you find that was miraculous? What does Helaman 12:13-17 add to our understanding? What miracles has God been willing to perform in your life so that you can be victorious?

In Joshua 10-11 there are several verses that document the destruction Israel unleashed upon these other nations. But here are a few verses that contain some marvelously phrased principles: Joshua 10:42, 11:6, 11:15, 11:18, and 11:23.

Day 152, Joshua 12-21

Joshua 12 lists all the kings that were defeated by Israel and Joshua. The only king left is the King of Kings and Lord of Lords.

To better visualize Joshua 13-21, find a map like Bible Map 3 that shows the division of the Twelve Tribes. What does Joshua 21:43-45 say about why they would spend nine chapters on dividing up the land?

In addition to the land, Caleb received Mount Hebron as an inheritance in Joshua 14. When we wholly follow the Lord, like Caleb, then we can take on challenges and adversity, and overcome them. They, then become inheritances for us through all of eternity (Joshua 14:8-14). "Give me this mountain," first as a challenge, and then as an inheritance (:12).

Not all of the tribes had received an inheritance at this point. In Joshua 18:3, note the prophets' pointed counsel to them. Why don't we go and obtain all the blessings promised to us?

Joshua 21 outlines how the Levites would receive 48 cities within the inheritances of the other tribes. What lessons might God be teaching us about priesthood and those who hold it. Why do you think it is so important to have priesthood in every family, home, town, stake, and country?

Day 153, Joshua 22-23

As the tribes of Reuben, Gad, and half of Manasseh returned to the land of their inheritance, on the East side of the Jordan River, Joshua gave his departing counsel to them in Joshua 22:1-6. When these tribes arrived in their land, they built an altar (Joshua 22:10). Fearing the two and a half tribes had turned to idolatry with this new altar, the other tribes marshalled their forces to confront them (Joshua 22:11-20). The two and a half tribes offered up their defense a reasoning for building the altar in verses 21-29. Why did they build the altar (:26-28)?

This chapter is a wonderful example about how families and individuals should solve disputes. Both sides explained their side of the conflict and because of careful listening, love and understanding was kindled (:29-34). Are their individuals that you need to understand better so your desire to have conflict with them will be diminished and replaced with love and respect?

Joshua was getting old (23:1). As part of his concluding counsel, he taught Israel about what to cleave to, and what not to cleave to in verses 2-13. To what things do you need to cleave in your life? To what things do you need to stop cleaving? Elder Neal A. Maxwell said, "God asks us to give up those things which, if clung to, will destroy us" (Ensign, Nov 1974).

If God blesses us when we are good, He will also curse us when we are bad (Joshua 23:14-16).

Day 154, Joshua 24

In verses 2-11, God reminded Israel of all that He did for them. You may want to mark the word "I" as you read. What would be on your personalized list if God were just speaking to you?

Because of everything the Lord has done for us and Israel we should follow the counsel in verses 14-15.

Look in verses 14-24 for how important it is that we serve the Lord. How is service a sign that we have "inclined [our] heart unto the God of Israel" (:23)?

What does Joshua do in verses 25-27 to help the people remember their covenant others the Lord? What reminders do you have of the covenants you have made?

Day 155, Judges 1-2

Identify what the children of Israel asked the Lord in Judges 1:1 after Joshua's death. In verses 2-18, the tribe of Judah, with the help of others, conquered for a time. Then, in verse 19, look for the thing that stopped them. Are there excuses you make for why you can't be obedient to the commandments?

As you read Judges 1:27-35, mark the words "neither," "nor," and anything else that shows they didn't drive out other inhabitants. How well do you drive out sin and other negative influences? Do you ever let them stay around and pay tribute (1:28)?

As you read Judges 2:1-15, look for how the Lord feels about the inhabitants not being driven out. What pattern was demonstrated, regarding how Israel responded to the judges sent by the Lord in Judges 2:7,10, and 16-19?

Driving out the former inhabitants was a test, and when they didn't drive them out the Lord used those people to test Israel (Judges 2:20-23). Thus, the Lord can teach us lessons regardless any circumstances.

Day 156, Judges 3

When the children of Israel did wickedly, the Lord raised up nations to provoke them. When they cried for help, the Lord would raise up a righteous judge to save them (Judges 3:6-11). One of these judges was Ehud. As a left-handed man from the tribe of Benjamin, he would have been viewed as an unlikely deliverer (:15). Ehud made a dagger that was a cubit long (:16). Most daggers are not this big. A cubit is from the tip of the middle finger to the elbow. That is about 18 inches. Look in verse 17 to see why he needed such a long dagger. In verses 18-25, you will read about how Ehud delivered Israel from Eglon in a fun and disgusting way. Here are a few of principles we can learn from this story:

- Big problems require big solutions.
- It is important to have the right tool.

- Big sin requires big repentance.

If God can use a left-handed man to be a deliverer, he can also use you. If you have an Eglon-sized problem in your life, what are some of the things that you feel you must do to be delivered from it?

Day 157, Judges 4-5

When Ehud died, so did the faithfulness of the people (Judges 4:1). Their belief was based upon proximity. Are you the type of person that when others are around you, they do better or worse?

After the people were tormented by the Canaanites, the Lord provided Deborah and Barak to deliver them. What qualities of leadership can you see in the prophetess in Judges 4:2-14?

As the battle raged, Sisera, king of Canaan, fled on foot. Read Judges 4:15-24 to discover the great actions of another incredible woman. How might God use you to deliver and aid His people? This story also highlights this great principle: Don't be alone in a room with a person of the opposite sex; you might get nailed.

Day 158, Judges 6

Look for what happened to Israel in verses 1-5 when Deborah was no longer leading them. When Israel cried unto God for help in verses 6-7, look for what He reminded them of in verses 8-10. How many of your own problems do you feel are self-inflicted?

The dialogue between Gideon and an angel in verses 11-24 is wonderful. As you study it, look for great lines, questions, excuses, and miracles. When the Lord asks you to do things, do you often come up with a list about why you wouldn't be the right person? Why do you think the Lord keeps calling people to save His people who feel inadequate?

Look for what the Lord had Gideon do in verses 25-40 to start turning people away from the worship of false gods and back to Him. Check out footnote 25b for more understanding. What do you think are some of the false altars that need to be cut down in our day? What fleece-type miracles has God given to you, so that you know He will save and help you (:34-40)?

Day 159, Judges 7

The Lord promised Gideon that He would deliver Israel through his leadership. Gideon amassed such a large force that the Lord was concerned the people would think they saved themselves (:1-2). What is a potential danger if people believe they can always save themselves?

As you read verses 3-25, look for how the Lord systematically depleted Gideon's army and miraculously proved He was the true Savior of Israel. Do you think the men who were excused after the second sifting might have felt unworthy? If they were able and willing, but not called, how should they have felt? What are some situations today where people might need to be reminded that they are still worthy, even though they were not called?

Verse 21 states, "And they stood every man in his place." We all have a part to play. Sometimes we are in the battle and sometimes we are not. Where is God asking you to make a stand right now?

Day 160, Judges 8-9

In Judges 8:1-21, Gideon tracked down and destroyed the Midianites. He then inflicted justice upon those who refused to help him. After winning many battles, it is no wonder the people wanted to make him their ruler. Look for how Gideon responded to their request in Judges 8:22-23. How will you submit your liberty over to the rule or will of God today?

To remind the people of their submission to God, Gideon collected their God and molded a golden ephod for the priests to wear, but it had a corruptible influence and the people began to worship it (Judges 8:24-27, 27a). Not more than four verses after warning them to let God rule their lives, the people again turned to the worship of an idol. It is no wonder that when Gideon died, so did their faithfulness (Judges 8:33-35). What will you do so that your faith and faithfulness isn't dependent upon others? What will you do so that others' faith and faithfulness isn't dependent upon you?

Abimelech was one of Gideon's sons. In Judges 9, we get the tragic and humorous tale of his life. Seeking for leadership, he killed all his brothers. Then, while seeking to subdue those who opposed him, he is killed in a battle. The circumstances of his death are great and can be found in Judges 9:45-57).

Day 161, Judges 10-12

In Judges 10:1-6, we will find more proximity-based faithfulness with the deaths of the judges Tola and Jair. When they died, so did obedience. In Judges 10:10-16, there was a great back and forth discussion between the Lord and the children of Israel. In verses 13-14, the Lord told them to go and pray to their fake Gods for help. The false Gods that take our time, money, talents, and love have no power to hear our prayers and deliver us from our problems. What kind of back-and-forth dialogue do you think the Lord would have with His people today?

As the son of a harlot, Jephthah had no claim on any inheritance and was another unlikely hero (Judges 11:1-6). He made a rash oath to defeat the Ammonites, which resulted in the sacrifice of his daughter (Judges 11:29-40). This is a little weird. Most scholars believe she made a vow to remain a virgin instead of being killed.

In Judges 12:1-6, the Ephraimites were upset because they were not invited to the battle against the Ammonites and, thus, denied the spoils of war. Seeking revenge, they came to fight the Gileadites, who slayed 42,000 Ephraimites. As the Ephraimites were fleeing, the Gileadites took control of the passes and would ask them to say the word "shibboleth." Those who were unable to do so, and could only say "sibboleth," were detected and destroyed. Each of us must pass our own test to prove our real identity. In a very real way, we are asked daily to identify our true selves. The world and God wants to know if we can say "shibboleth."

Day 162, Judges 13-15

In Judges 13:1-8, Manoah and his wife were barren but an angel appeared and promised that their son would have great power (:5). The angel also told them to make their son, Samson, a Nazarite (:4-5, and Numbers 6). That means no wine, no meat, no haircuts, and no touching dead bodies—all in addition to the regular commandments. Watch for how many of these covenants and commandments Samson broke.

In Judges 14:1-4, Samson wanted to marry a Philistine filly outside of the covenant. What is the problem with that? Then, in Judges 14:5-9, look for what he did and who he didn't tell. In Judges 14:10-20, you will find Samson's wedding, a riddle, and a massacre. The wording found in Judges 14:19 was the author's way of pointing out that Samson's strength came from the Lord, but not His approval.

In Judges 15:1-8, you get a story of revenge, revenge, and revenge. When the Philistines came to capture Samson, look for the miraculous display of his power and the Lord's protection in verses 10-20. From what you have read, would you say that Samson is powerful, or weak? How was he doing on keeping his covenants?

Day 163, Judges 16-21

How does the story in Judges 16:1-3 demonstrate Samson's power and weakness? In Judges 16:4-16, we are introduced to Delilah, Samson's love for her, and her betrayals. Why do you think Samson stayed with her? If you were Samson's friend, what advice would you give to him?

Look in Judges 16:16 to discover why he finally gave in. You don't have to give in to daily temptations (Genesis 39:10-12). What will you do to make sure you avoid becoming like Samson? Samson's story ended in Judges 16:17-31. Why do you think the Lord gave Samson his power back? What does the story of Samson teach you about power and covenants?

The stories in Judges 17-21 are to prove the truthfulness of Judges 17:6 and 21:25. What has the book of Judges taught you about the importance of leadership?

Day 164, Ruth 1

Ruth was a convert to the church. As you read verses 1-15, look for all the challenges that came to her young faith. What are some of the usual challenges that come to new members in our day?

When many others would have faltered and given up, look for how Ruth kept her faith and her covenants in verses 16-17. How does she compare to Samson?

When your life and plans are destroyed, do you, like Ruth, go to Bethlehem to find a Savior (:18-22)? The story of Ruth is the story of how God repairs lives when they look destroyed.

Day 165, Ruth 2

As you read this chapter, watch for places where Ruth served, worked, trusted in God, and went forward with faith. How might those same principles provide the solution to most to the difficult circumstances that we find ourselves in?

Just as Ruth is fantastic, so is Boaz. Boaz did all that was required by the law and more to help take care of those in need (:8-9, and 14-16). What is so impressive about a person who has means, who really helps the poor?

Here, "one of our next kinsmen" refers to redeemer (:20b). "The word here rendered 'redeemer' we translate literally from Hebrew go'el and this is its proper translation. It is rendered merely 'kinsman' in the King James English translation. The function of a go'el was to make it possible for a widow who had lost home and property to return to her former status and security and to have seed to perpetuate her family. It is easy to see why the later prophets borrowed this word from the social laws of Israel and used it to describe the functions of Him who would become the Divine Redeemer: Think of what He does to restore us to proper status with God, and to give us future security and eternal 'seed'" (*Old Testament Student Manual*: Genesis–2 Samuel. Church Educational System manual, p. 263).

Day 166, Ruth 3

Ruth visited Boaz to notify him that he was to be the redeemer, the *go'el*, by uncovering his feet and laying there (:1-9). The symbolism of uncovering Boaz' feet was to let him know there was something left undone or unattended. Ruth was uncovered and unprotected.

This beautiful story "speaks of and symbolically demonstrates God's redeeming power; it teaches us of how we can access that power and exemplifies how we should emulate our Redeemer. Numerous elements of the story serve as types of Christ. It is about hope in Israel. [Perhaps part of] the reason we love the story so much is because … our souls intuitively resonate with the redemption of Ruth; we long for what happened to her on a mortal level to happen to us in both a mortal and eternal way. Ruth satisfies some of our soul's yearning for deliverance. It highlights our reasons for hope" (Kerry Muhlestein, "Ruth, Redemption, Covenant, and Christ," in D. Kelly Ogden, Jared W. Ludlow, and Kerry Muhlstein, eds., The Gospel of Jesus Christ in the Old Testament, 38th Annual Brigham Young University Sidney B. Sperry Symposium [2009], 187–88).

"The man will not rest, until he have finished the thing this day" (:18). May we be as eager and committed in carrying out the redemption of others that lies within our power.

Day 167, Ruth 4

It was through the attempt of many to keep their covenants that God had kept His covenant (:14-15). Each person is an expression of God's efforts to bless His children. Who do you think is the best example of the Savior in this story: Ruth, Naomi, or Boaz?

The message of Ruth is simple: God does not leave us without a redeemer.

Day 168, 1 Samuel 1

Write down the words "prayer," "parenthood," and "priesthood." As you study this chapter, list the great truths that you learn about each of these topics. Try to find a couple of truths for each topic.

Keep your list so you can add to it tomorrow.

Day 169, 1 Samuel 2

In verses 1-10, Hannah offered up a prayer of gratitude for her child. How do your prayers of thanksgiving compare? For which blessings do you need to take time to really express your love and appreciation to God?

As you make your way through verses 11-36, discover some additional truths that you could list under the topics of parenthood and priesthood.

Day 170, 1 Samuel 3

Search verses 1-10 for all the subtle things you can discover about listening to the voice of the Lord. Then answer some of the following questions:

- What words did the Lord use when calling Samuel? Why is that significant?
- Why do you think Samuel thought it was Eli? What does that teach us about the voice of the Lord?
- Why do you think the Lord called Samuel and not Eli? What does that tell us about Samuel and ourselves if we want to hear?
- What lesson can we learn from the fact that Samuel had to answer the Lord before the Lord continued with his message?
- How many times did God call? Why so often?
- What can we learn from Samuel's example in how he responded?

In verses 11-14, Samuel learned that Eli was going to be replaced. He was afraid to tell Eli (:15). Eli asked Samuel about what the Lord said and asked him not to hide it; Samuel doesn't (:16-18). Prophets reveal, they don't conceal. What else can we learn about prophets from verses 19-21?

Day 171, 1 Samuel 4

As you read verses 1-11, look for how people placed their fear and faith in the Ark of the Covenant, rather than in God. The Israelites thought that just having the Ark—or the appearance of righteousness—would be enough to secure victory. What could be some of the problems of trying to appear more righteous than we really are?

In verses 12-22, you will find the fulfillment of the prophecy made about Eli and his sons in 1 Samuel 3:11-14. Why do you think it is important to know that God is as just as He is merciful?

Day 172, 1 Samuel 5

After the Philistines won the battle, what might they have thought about the God of Israel and the Ark of the Covenant? What might the Philistines have thought about their god Dagon in comparison to Jehovah?

Look for what happened in this chapter to convince the Philistines that Jehovah really is God. You will also need to find out what an *emerod* is by using footnote 6a.

In the last chapter Israel pretended to be powerful when they were spiritually pitiful, and the Philistines won. What has God taught the Philistines about Himself? Finish the following sentence: "Israel or the Church may be wicked but God is…"

Day 173, 1 Samuel 6-7

Some Philistines might have said the experiences of the last chapter were just bad luck or coincidences. To make sure they were not overreacting, the Philistines created a test to find out if the God of Israel really was God. Note the parameters and results of this test in 1 Samuel 6:1-16. What were some of the experiences that convince you God is in the details of coincidence? In 1 Samuel 6:19-20, you will see that Israel was not worthy of the Ark either; they were no better than Philistines. God is real and powerful, even if His people are not.

Taking the Ark of the Covenant into battle was an attempt to look more righteous than they were (1 Samuel 4). Look in 1 Samuel 7:3-13 for what Israel did this time to make sure that the Lord was going to be with them. What changed when Israel became as righteous as they appeared? What do you think would be a good way to finish the following statement? "If I am not what I seem to be, then I should…"

Day 174, 1 Samuel 8

What problems did the sons of Samuel create for the people of Israel in verses 1-5?

Look in verses 6-9 to discover the Lord's feelings about Israel's decision. Which modern-day issues do you think make those feelings reemerge?

What warnings did Samuel give about kings in verses 10-18? Remember this warning as we study the lives of the kings.

According to verses 5, 19-22, what were the reasons that Israel wanted a king? What are some issues, standards, or doctrines that modern day members sometimes want to change so that we can be like other people? What do you think is the real problem if we spend our time and effort to become like the rest of the world? Is there anything in your life where you feel the Lord would want you to follow Him rather than the world?

Day 175, 1 Samuel 9

As you read about Saul in this chapter, look closely for the qualities of a righteous king/leader. As you read about Samuel, look for the qualities of a "seer." You may want to make a list and mark the word "seer" as you study.

What were the things that Samuel heard and saw that others could not? What are the things that modern-day seers are seeing and hearing? What are some of the current stories you have heard about any of the fifteen men we sustain as prophets, seers, and revelators, which show similar qualities to those demonstrated by Samuel?

Day 176, 1 Samuel 10

When kings are doing what they should, they become powerful symbols of Jesus Christ (:1). Do you allow the Lord and His righteous leaders to "captain" your soul and life, or do you still wrestle them for control (:1)? What results have you witnessed when others mutiny against the Lord?

Which of the lines of hymn number 104 do you think would be a good cross-reference for this verse?

Look for the miracles that are foretold and fulfilled in verses 2-16 as a confirming witness to Saul that his calling and anointing came from God. In which of your callings have you felt the sustaining hand of heaven? When have you felt that a calling turned you into another person, or gave you a new heart (:6, and 9).

What do you love about the announcement of Saul being anointed king by Samuel in verses 17-27? In what ways might people avoid service today by hiding among "stuff" (:22)?

Day 177, 1 Samuel 11-12

The Ammonites sought to force Jabesh into submission (1 Samuel 11:1-3). Jabesh, appealed to Israel and their new king for help. In verses 4-11, look for how Saul responded, the object lesson he used, and the details of the battle. After the victory, those who refused to sustain Saul with gift are threatened with their lives (1 Samuel 10:27, and 11:12). Saul demonstrated two incredible qualities in his response. First, he was merciful, and second, he gave God credit for the win (1 Samuel 11:13).

After winning the battle against the Ammonites, the people of Israel may have been tempted to think that Samuel and the Lord were wrong for not wanting them to have a king. In 1 Samuel 12, Samuel gave the people a talk about how there would not be a problem if the people and King Saul would keep the commandments, but if they didn't keep the commandments there would be problems. Verses 12-25 are the best. Find some lines that are worth marking and remembering.

Day 178, 1 Samuel 13

1 Samuel chapters 9-11 show how the Lord enhanced and blessed Saul. 1 Samuel 13-15 show why Saul was rejected by the Lord. Today, we begin the study of the fall of Saul.

The Philistines came to battle because Jonathan conquered a garrison (:1-3). The Israelites used farm equipment for weapons, which, ironically enough, was sharpened by the Philistines. There were only two swords in the Israelite army (:19-23). As the people of Israel fled into caves, thickets, and other land, the people were trembling with fear (:4-7).

To make this stressful situation worse, Samuel the prophet was running late (:8). As you study verses 8-14, look for Saul's mistake, the excuses that Saul gave, and the correction of Samuel. What would have happened if Saul had waited just a little longer (:10)? How often are excuses, like those in verses 11-12, offered by those who break commandments? When we break the commandments because of excuses, we qualify to receive the same correction offered in verses 13-14.

Day 179, 1 Samuel 14-15

Jonathan, the son of Saul, was an incredibly courageous and faithful man. He would have been a tremendous king. Read the story of Jonathan defeating an entire Philistine garrison in 1 Samuel 14:1-15. Is this act any less distinguished than David's defeat of Goliath a few chapters later? There should be no reason to feel any less important or capable if someone else is called to a leadership position and we are not. In 1 Samuel 14:16-52, Saul almost has Jonathan killed to fulfill a dumb oath.

What commandment did king Saul receive from the Lord in 1 Samuel 15:1-3? Look for how well Saul did at obeying that command as you read 1 Samuel 15:4-9.

There are a ton of principles about obedience, disobedience, sacrifice, and repentance in 1 Samuel 16:10-35. Read these verses and try to mark several of these lessons.

Day 180, 1 Samuel 16

When people prove themselves unworthy of positions they hold, the Lord begins to prepare their replacements (:1). What did the Lord teach Samuel about appearances and how He judges people in verses (:2-13)? How can the truth about the Lord's judgment, mentioned in verse 7, be comforting and terrifying?

What can you learn about how music can affect our actions, thoughts, and spirituality from the story in verses 14-23? Check out the helpful JST footnotes 14c, 15a, and 16a. How do you, or how could you use sacred music to court the Spirit of the Lord and fight off evil thoughts and feelings?

Day 181, 1 Samuel 17:1-41

Look in verses 1-11 for what made Goliath such a terrifying adversary. What are some of the large and challenging situations that you are facing?

What lessons can you learn from verses 12-40 about how to prepare temporally and spiritually so that you might "draw near" to the challenges you will face with faith and not fear (:40)?

Look in verses 34-37 for the experiences that helped David feel confident to battle Goliath. What experiences have built your confidence that God will help you with your struggles?

Why do you think David decided to use the weapons that had worked well for him in the past instead of those things which he had "not proved" (:39-40)?

Day 182, 1 Samuel 17:42-58

Read verses 42-44, looking for how Goliath saw David and his God. Why do you think people sometimes think that those who believe in God are weaklings?

Read verses 45-47, and look for how David viewed himself and his God. Who do you think trashed talked better: David or Goliath?

How do you think David's confidence in God in verses 45-47 helped him to approach Goliath in verses 48-51? Notice the speed at which David approached Goliath in those verses. When we approach problems with faith in God, the problems often fall or flee away.

How did David's faith and actions affect the Philistines and Israelites in verses 47-58?

Day 183, 1 Samuel 18

Look for how Jonathan, the son of Saul felt about David in verses 1-4. Now, look in verses 5-8 to discover how Saul felt about David.

> There are going to be times in our lives when someone else gets an unexpected blessing or receives some special recognition. May I plead with us not to be hurt—and certainly not to feel envious—when good fortune comes to another person? We are not diminished when

someone else is added upon. We are not in a race against each other. … The race we are really in is the race against sin, and surely envy is one of the most universal of those (Jeffrey R. Holland "The Laborers in the Vineyard," Ensign or Liahona, May 2012, 31).

Look for all the foolish choices in verses 9-30 that came because of jealously. Pride prevents us from being happy when others are successful. Are there people for whom you need to start cheering and stop being jealous? Can you be a good follower when you are not the leader?

While others were making poor choices, David "behaved himself wisely" (:5, 14-15, 30). Will you behave wisely today?

Day 184, 1 Samuel 19-21

Look for how the friendship of Jonathan and the support of Michal and Ahimelech helped David in 1 Samuel 19-21. As you read these chapters, look for verses that contain phrases of friendship and love.

What difference does the love and support of friends and family make in your life? Who has been your Jonathan during your life?

Day 185, 1 Samuel 22-24

As you read 1 Samuel 22-24, look for the difference between how Saul and David treat the Lord's anointed. Why do you think David chose to treat Saul as the Lord's anointed, even when he had been ordained by Samuel to become king?

How do you treat the Lord's anointed? Do you look for and dwell on their flaws? Do you support and sustain them?

Here are a few good verses to find some amazing principles: 1 Samuel 22:1-2, 22-23; and 1 Samuel 23:2-4, 14, 16.

Day 186, 1 Samuel 25

What happened in verses 1-13 that made David so angry that he roused his troops to attack?

As you study verses 14-31, look for ways that Abigail became a symbol for Christ in how she saved Nabal and David. Was the forgiveness for the benefit David or Nabal?

What blessings did David identify in verses 32-35 that came from Abigail's mediation?

Look for the rest of the story in verses 36-41.

Day 187, 1 Samuel 26-28

What is so remarkable about how David continued to see and treat Saul in chapter 26? How can David's example help us as we interact with family, friends, coworkers, and enemies?

Which of the following are acceptable sources of revelation: horoscopes, tarot cards, ouija boards, crystal balls, palm readers, patriarchal blessings, prayer, prophets, and scriptures? Search 1 Samuel 28 to see where Saul went for revelation. Why do you think some of these things are attractive to people? If we want real revelation from God, what must we do?

Day 188, 1 Samuel 29-31

As you read chapter 29, look for phrases that Achish said about David that you would like people who don't belong to the Church to say about you.

Search 1 Samuel 30 for all the ways that David sought for answers and information (:6) when he faced a problem that made him "greatly distressed." Looking broadly, in addition to looking heavenward, often allows the Lord to give us the eyes to see the solution. Are there any distressing situations for which you need search for more information?

After reading 1 Samuel 31, what gospel principles would you emphasize if you had to speak at the funeral of Saul and Jonathan?

Day 189, 2 Samuel 1-4

As you read 2 Samuel 1, watch for how David showed us how to morn over the mighty when they die. How do you think it is possible that David felt for Saul what he also felt for Jonathan?

Note what happened to each of the following individuals in 2 Samuel 2-4:

- David
- Ahinoam

- Abigail
- Ish-bosheth
- Abner
- Joab
- Asahel
- Michal
- Mephibosheth
- Rechab and Baanah

Which story shows kindness? Which story shows mercy? Which story shows justice? Which story shows the ugliness of war?

Day 190, 2 Samuel 5, and 8-10

As you read chapters 5, 8, and 10, look for the variety of things that David does to become a successful king and leader. What does 2 Samuel 5:1-4 say about how old David was when he became king, and how long did he reign?

In 2 Samuel 9, David showed great kindness to Mephibosheth, the son of Jonathan, who showed great kindness to David. I have often received the benefit of generational kindness through the friends of my parents and grandparents. When were times in your life that you gave or received generational kindness?

Day 191, 2 Samuel 6-7

When the Ark of the Covenant was constructed, Aaron and his sons received strict instructions not to touch the holy image that represented the throne of God (Numbers 4:15-20). Look for what happened when Uzzah steadied the Ark when it nearly fell during transportation in 2 Samuel 6:1-7. How does the Lord use symbolism here to teach what happens to those who think they can correct and save God? Who are some current examples of people or groups who are trying to correct, change, or save the Church and God from what they believe are mistakes?

In 2 Samuel 6:9-23, the Ark was brought to Jerusalem very carefully. What lessons about dancing did David and his wife, Michal, teach?

Draw a picture of a tent and a house. In which does David live (2 Samuel 7:2)? David desired to build a house for the Ark of the Covenant. Why hadn't the children of Israel built a temple yet? Why only a tabernacle?

What does it tell us, symbolically, that we build temples today and not tabernacles? How did the Lord respond to David's desire to build a temple in 2 Samuel 7:4-17?

Day 192, 2 Samuel 11

Up to this point, King David had been one of the greatest examples of righteousness in the Bible. Now, we are going to study the tragic event that cost this prophet-king his exaltation (D&C 132:39). As you study 2 Samuel 11, look for places were David could have—and should have—made a different choice.

Why do you think the people involved didn't stop what they were doing? When should it have stopped? When was it too late?

Rank the following people in order of most guilty to least guilty: Bath-Sheba, Joab, David, David's messengers, and Uriah.

What was the difference between the David who faced Goliath and the one who faced Bath-Sheba?

What have you learned so that you never lose your exaltation?

Day 193, 2 Samuel 12

Did David get away with adultery and murder? How many ways did David try to cover up his sin in yesterday's chapter?

Look for how Nathan the prophet used a story about a lamb to help David see his sins in verses 1-9. How open and bold does the Lord have to be with you to get you to repent? Does He have to send people to your house, or do you seek Him out? How can leaders and parents help people to quit hiding from the Lord and instead be healed?

There are always consequences for sin. Look for both the short- and long-term consequences that would come to David and his household in verses 10-24. Why is it better to repent and face consequences rather than to hide and receive punishment?

Day 194, 2 Samuel 13

As you read the story in verses 1-20, do you think this is a love or lust story? What is sad about verse 15?

Have you ever seen either one of the following cycles? Love leads to respect which leads to more love (Alma 38:9). Lust leads to disrespect which leads to hate (2 Samuel 13:15). Which cycle do you remember being manifest the most during your high school years? When the prophets teach dating standards and the law of chastity, how are they trying to increase our ability to love?

How common is the story of revenge and retaliation like that found in verses 21-38? We have all seen how someone's sin has led others to make mistakes while seeking to get even or ahead. Is there a mistake or sin of someone else where you need to leave judgment in the hands of God and move on?

Day 195, 2 Samuel 14-24

As you read chapter headings for 2 Samuel 14-24, look for how accurately the prophecy of Nathan to David in 2 Samuel 12:10-12 was fulfilled.

What does Absalom do in 2 Samuel 15 to win the hearts and confidence of the people? How could we use this same principle to win the hearts of our children?

As you read 2 Samuel 17, consider how important is it that other people take your advice.

What evidence is there in 2 Samuel 18-19 that wicked and rebellious children are stilled love by their parents?

Day 196, 1 Kings 1-3

1 Kings 1-2 contains the story of how Solomon was established as the next king following David. David told Solomon that great leaders are those who are great followers of God (1Kings 2:1-3).

In 1 Kings 3:1-15, look for what Solomon did so the Lord would grant unto him a great gift. For what gift did Solomon ask? How did the Lord feel about his request? For what kind of things do you ask God? For what gift might God want you to ask Him?

How does the story in 1 Kings 3:16-28 show that Solomon received the gift for which he asked God? What is so impressive about a king taking time to help solve a problem between two harlots? How is this a great symbol of Christ's ability to issue judgment?

Day 197, 1 Kings 4-7

Solomon's wisdom is celebrated in 1 Kings 4:29-34. What is the wisest thing the wisest man ever did? Check out the chapter headings of 1 Kings 5-8.

What are the best conditions for building temples according to 1 Kings 5:1-5? In much of chapters 5-7, Solomon procured the finest materials for the construction of the temple. What are some of the different purposes for building temples that are striking in their physical beauty?

What promises did the Lord make to His people in 1 Kings 6:11-13? How does the temple help fulfill this promise?

What do you think of when you see the wonderful part of the temple described in 1 Kings 7:23-26?

Day 198, 1 Kings 8-9

In 1 Kings 8:12-54, you will find the dedicatory prayer for the temple. What were some common themes you noticed as you read this sacred prayer? What do you think is the connection between the things prayed for during a temple dedication and the blessings that can be expected? Most modern-day temple blessings have been published by the Church in the Church News. Here is a challenge: See if you can find the dedicatory prayer for the temple in your temple district. You might want to do a Google search for something like "Manti temple dedicatory prayer." Read it, and then compare it with Solomon's. What did you find?

When a temple is dedicated, it still needs to be accepted. In 1 Kings 9:1-10, you will read how the Lord accepted Solomon's temple. Keep your eye out for a couple of great "if/then" promises that were made.

Day 199, 1 Kings 10-11

What evidence is there in 1 Kings 10:1-13 that Solomon was still sought out for his wisdom?

What evidence is there in 1 Kings 10:14-29 that Solomon was becoming obsessed with obtaining wealth?

What happened to Solomon's great wisdom in 1 Kings 11:1-13? What does this story teach us about how who we marry affects the spirituality of ourselves and our children?

Because of Solomon's choices, the Lord had Ahijah, the prophet, visit Jeroboam. As you read 1 Kings 11:28-43, note what Ahijah did to Jeroboam's coat. What did it mean? If people do not follow the Lord's direction on marriage, He will remove kingdoms from them.

Day 200, 1 Kings 12

King Rehoboam was in need of counseling. As you read verses 1-15, look for the diverse groups that offered their advice. Why do you think Rehoboam listened to the group that he did? Who are the groups that are trying to give you counsel? What did Rehoboam misunderstand about leadership and service?

We have already watched King Rehoboam make a political blunder, now it is time for Jeroboam to make one. The people of Israel had to travel to the temple to make sacrifices. Jeroboam was fearful that this would eventually turn the hearts of the people back to Rehoboam. Look what Jeroboam offered the people in place of true temple worship in verses 25-33. What are ways in which you have seen people replace the temple with other things?

Day 201, 1 Kings 13

How many notable things do you see happening in verses 1-10?

What does the story found in verses 11-32 teach you about obedience? This story is further complicated by the JST footnote 18b. Why is it important not to let anyone talk us out of doing what we know to be right?

You have just finished reading about the illustrious standards that the Lord has for His prophets. Now, check out how Jeroboam responded to their ministry and the quality of priests that he appointed in verses 33-34.

Day 202, 1 Kings 14

What is a blind prophet able to see and hear that others can't in verses 1-20? It is possible for a person to lie his or her way through a temple recommend interview, but there are occasions when the Lord whispers warnings to His servants, or gives them eyes to see what is really there.

Within five years of replacing his father, King Solomon, Rehoboam had led Judah into terrible wickedness. Check out verses 21-24 and 24a. In verses 25-27 you will see how Rehoboam traded in the golden shields that Solomon crafted for brass shields. Often the world comes at us offering to trade us brass for gold. Our standards and temple blessings are gold, yet we are offered brass by the world for breaking them. Don't pay your tithing and save 10 percent: brass. Pay your tithing and keep the temples, chapels, and blessings: gold. Experience a fleeting moment of pleasure: brass. A sealed marriage: gold. Every day the world offers us brass for gold. When this happens today, you may want to repeat this phrase: "I will not trade my gold for brass."

Day 203, 1 Kings 15-16

In 1 Kings 15:1-15, you will see how Abijam and Asa—two brothers and kings of Judah—behaved themselves very differently. We know they were brothers because of 1 Kings 15:2 and 10. There is more to this relationship. Check out 1 Kings 15:8. As part of the fertility worship of the false god Baal and Asherah—or Ashtaroth—Abijam sired a son with his own mother. Being born into these type of circumstances is what makes Asa's actions in 1 Kings 15:9-14 so awesome. If Asa was righteous in those conditions, what about us?

Baasha is the king of Israel that replaced Nadab, son of Jeroboam. How did Baasha come to obtain his power, according to 1 Kings 15:25-30? Then, notice what the Lord asked the prophet Jehu to speak against Baasha in 1 Kings 16:1-7. You should be getting the idea that the lives of these kings would play out like a soap opera. To help you keep track of which kings are over Judah and which are over Israel, you can go to the "Chronology" in the Bible Dictionary. In the rest of 1 Kings 16, you will learn about Elah, Zimri, Omri, and Ahab. You may want to make a note next to each name in the Chronology about whether they were righteous or wicked.

Day 204, 1 Kings 17

In verse 1, we see that Elijah had the sealing power and used it to stop rain and dew. This area of Israel gets several inches of dew each year, making it an important staple in their water supply.

Which of the two feedings of the prophet Elijah most impresses you: the one in verses 2-8 or the one in verses 9-16? In what ways will our homes be blessed as we exercise similar faith in the Lord's prophets?

Following the astonishing feeding of the widow and her son was a devastating event and miracle in verses 17-24. Do you know people who have gone through a tragedy and are still able to say what was said in verse 24?

Day 205, 1 Kings 18:1-29

A meeting between king Ahab and Elijah was arranged in verses 1-16, but if you read it carefully you will also learn of some other miraculous things.

Look for who Ahab and Elijah blamed for the drought and famine in verses 17-18. Who was right? In what ways do people claim that prophets cause trouble in our day?

In verses 19-29, you will find the first part of the "Whose God is God?" test. What did the worshippers of Baal do in an attempt to gain his attention? Sex worship was another customary practice among those who sought to worship Baal. They employed the services of male or female prostitutes to perform actions before an idol. This was done with a hope that Baal would then impregnate his wife, Ashtoreth, resulting in blessings of rain and harvest. Baalism is alive and well in our society today. Satan has changed it from being a religion to a culture. He still seeks to get his followers to harm the human body and to expose it.

Day 206, 1 Kings 18:30-46

Yesterday we read about the failed attempts of the priests of Baal to prove the power and reality of their god. In verses 30-39, you will see the difference between God and Baal. Baal was also the god of the sun and fire, which makes this test even more convincing.

The tremendous power that was shown from heaven on this occasion is proof of God. But there is another detail that also showed the greatness of God. Look for Elijah and God's purpose for doing this test in verses 36-37. After all of the Baal things these people had done, God and His prophet still sought to bring them back. That is the real proof and test of a God. He still wants us, even though we have been with Baal. What proofs have you had of God in your life that have cause you to react like those in verse 39?

What two other miracles are mentioned in verses 40-46? The town Jezebel is about 26 miles away from mount Carmel, where the sacrifices occurred.

Day 207, 1 Kings 19

As you read verses 1-10, note how Ahab, Jezebel, and Elijah respond after the incredible miracles in the last chapter.

To show Elijah that miracles don't convince or convert people, the Lord gave Elijah an experience with the wind, an earthquake, a fire, and the Holy Ghost (:11-12). Look for what the following quote can teach you about the still small voice of the spirit:

> That sweet, quiet voice of inspiration comes more as a feeling than it does as a sound. Pure intelligence can be spoken into the mind. The Holy Ghost communicates with our spirits through the mind more than through the physical senses [see 1 Corinthians 2:14; D&C 8:2; 9:8–9]. This guidance comes as thoughts, as feelings through promptings and impressions [see D&C 11:13; 100:5]....This process is not reserved for the prophets alone. The gift of the Holy Ghost operates equally with men, women, and even little children. It is within this wondrous gift and power that the spiritual remedy to any problem can be found....You can know the things you need to know. Pray that you will learn to receive that inspiration and remain worthy to receive it. Keep that channel—your mind—clean and free from the clutter of the world (Boyd K. Packer "Prayer and Promptings," Ensign Nov. 2009, 44-45).

What did Elijah learn in verses 13-18 about Hazel, Jesus, Elisha, and 7,000 others?

How willingly did Elisha accept his new calling in verses 19-21?

Day 208, 1 Kings 20-21

In an attempt to teach both Ahab and Syria that the God of Israel is the Lord, the Lord had a prophet proclaim that Israel would defeat Syria in battle when Syria threatened Israel (1 Kings 20:13, 23, and 28). Israel's army defeated Syria twice, but Ahab refused to kill Ben-hadad, the king of Syria. The Lord said Ahab would be replaced as king of Israel (:42). Notice how Ahab felt after his failure to follow a prophet's counsel in 1 Kings 20:43.

In 1 Kings 21:1-16, Ahab wanted a vineyard that belonged to Naboth, but Naboth wouldn't sell it. Look for what Jezebel did so Ahab could receive what he desired. Then, in verses 17-29, Elijah came to confront Ahab about his actions. Ahab was so confused, he thought the person who encouraged wickedness was his friend, Jezebel, and the prophet, who really did care about him, was his enemy (:20). In what ways do people make this same misjudgment today?

Day 209, 1 Kings 22

Look for the prophecies that Elijah made about Ahab and Jezebel in 1Kings 21:21-23. Then, read the chapter headings for 1 Kings 22 and 2 Kings 9 to find the fulfillment of these prophecies.

As the armies of Israel and Judah prepared a joint campaign against Syria, Ahab relied on his false prophets; but Jehoshaphat desired the word of a "prophet of the Lord" (:7). Look for the reason that Ahab disliked the prophet Miciah in verse 8. Do you trust and seek out the teaching and counsel of prophets like Jehoshaphat?

When the prophet Miciah's counsel was sought, look for what he said he would speak in verse 14. What evidence have you seen that the prophets of today are following this same rule? What happened to Miciah when he spoke for the Lord in verses 24-27?

Ahab tried to disguise himself to avoid a twice-prophesied punishment (:30). People often try to disguise themselves or their actions when they are doing wrong. Notice the difference between Ahab and Jehoshaphat in verses 41-50.

Day 210, 2 Kings 1

When Ahaziah became sick in verses 1-8, look to whom did he turned for help and to whom he did not turn. We are a people who know there is a God, prophets, and priesthood. Why do you think people who know these things sometimes turn away from the help they offer and, instead, turn toward other sources?

How did the messenger of Ahaziah describe Elijah in verse 8? Other than commenting on his physical appearance, what words would you use to describe the prophet Elijah? What words would you like people to use when describing you?

What else happened in verses 9-18 to further convince people that there was a God in Israel and that He called men to be His prophets? Will the still small voice work for you, or do you need fire from heaven to convince you of God and His prophets?

Day 211, 2 Kings 2

What kind of example of sticking with and following the prophet did Elisha set for us to follow in verses 1-6?

What does the story in verses 9-14 teach you about the transition of power that occurs from one prophet to another?

To understand why Elijah was translated and taken into heaven, you might want to look up "Elijah" and "Transfiguration, Mount of" in the Bible Dictionary. How has the translation of Elijah become a meaningful event in your life?

How does the prophet Elisha demonstrate the power to bless and curse in verses 19-24? Footnote 23a is worth looking at. Does your belief in and language toward God's prophets cause the power of heaven to be demonstrated in blessings or curses?

Day 212, 2 Kings 3-4

Today we will read several of the miracles that the prophet Elisha performed. As you read each section, write down the corresponding miracle.

- 2 Kings 3:11-24
- 2 Kings 4:1-7
- 2 Kings 4:8-17
- 2 Kings 4:18-37
- 2 Kings 4:38-41
- 2 Kings 4:42-44

Which of these miracles was your favorite? Elder Neal A. Maxwell said to "expect a miracle everyday" ("Jesus the Perfect Mentor." Ensign, February 2001, 8). What mini-miracle did God give to you yesterday or today?

Day 213, 2 Kings 5:1-13

How did the little missionary maid show tremendous faith in verses 1-5? How was the king of Israel's faith in verses 6-8?

How did Elisha test the faith of Naaman in verses 9-13? In what ways can big sacrifices be easier than little ones? What little thing should you be doing that would improve you? Why haven't you started doing it yet? What do you think Naaman's servant would tell you?

Day 214, 2 Kings 5:14-27

What does verse 14 teach you about strict obedience?

If Elisha would have come out and called down the power of heaven to heal Naaman as expected, how might verse 15 have read differently? How did the performance of this miracle glorify God and not just His prophet?

What is the powerful lesson about priestcraft to be learned from the story in verses 16-27? God is not an egomaniac; why does He want us to give the credit and glory to Him?

Day 215, 2 Kings 6

What does the remarkable miracle in verses 1-7 teach us about what types things are important enough for the Lord to care about?

What does the story in verses 8-23 teach you about the hearing, vision, and power of prophets? When was the last time God gave you the eyes to see that those who are with you are more than those that are against you (:16)? Why do you think it is important to remember that you have numbers on your side?

Verses 24-33 contain a sad story of two women. The king of Israel blamed Elisha rather than the women. Not only were the women to blame, but Moses warned of this very thing in prophetic manner years earlier (:29a). These women were unfamiliar with the scriptures and it cost them dearly.

Day 216, 2 Kings 7-9

Israel was in the midst of a famine caused by the invasion and siege of Syria. In 2 Kings 7:1-2, Elisha proclaimed that the next day the famine would be over and food would be had in abundance. The next day, four lepers found the Syria camp abandoned. What lesson about prophets and their words did the people learn in 2 Kings 7:16-20? What experience have you had that taught you the same thing?

Look for how obedience, coupled with impeccable timing of the Lord, led to a great miracle for the Shunamite women in 2 Kings 8:1-6. What did Elisha prophecy about Ben-hadad and Hazel in 2 Kings 8:7-15? How did Jehoram's marriage impact his life in 2 Kings 8:16-18?

In 2 Kings 9, we get another example of prophetic foresight. Check out the chapter heading. There is also gruesome gore in verses 30-37. Do you feel that is a fitting end to one who ended the lives of so many prophets?

Day 217, 2 Kings 10-13

In 2 Kings 10:1-28, Jehu slayed the sons of Ahab and the priests of Baal. The story of Baal's priests is great in verses 18-28. Note what Jehu said people could learn from these stories in verse 10 and 10a. Notice that Jehu could eradicate sin in others but not totally in himself (:29-31). How could the story of Jehu be like a returned missionary who becomes inactive?

Despite grandma Athaliah's attempts, Joash (Jehoash), with the help of the priest Jehoiada, renews the covenants of God with the tribe and people of Judah in 2 Kings 11. Verses 17-21 contain the great destruction of Baal worship. How can you be like Jehoiada and help others make covenants with God? In 2 Kings 12:2, Jehoash continued to listen to the instruction of the priests. He then used the donated money of the people to repair the temple. Jehoash even used funds to secure peace with Syria (2 Kings 12:18). What would you be willing to give up in order to have the blessings of the temple and peace in your life?

How is it that Jehoahaz, the king of Israel, was able to obtain help from the Lord, even though he was not perfect (2 Kings 13:1-6)? How cool was Elisha when he performed a miracle even though he was dead? What? I know! Check it out in 2 Kings 13:20-21.

Day 218, 2 Kings 14-16:4

In these chapters, the kings of Israel and Judah are paraded before us in rapid fire succession. As you look up each king, see what you can determine about their righteousness and influence.

- Amaziah, king of Judah (2 Kings 14:1-6)
- Jeroboam, king of Israel (2 Kings 14:23-24)
- Azariah/Uzziah, king of Judah (2 Kings 15:1-5)
- Zachariah, king of Israel (2 Kings 15:8-10)
- Shallum and Menahem, kings of Israel (2 Kings 15:13-18)
- Pekahiah, king of Israel (2 Kings 15:23-25)
- Pekah, king of Israel (2 Kings 15:27-28)
- Jotham, king of Judah (2 Kings 15:32-35)
- Ahab, king of Judah (2 Kings 16:1-4)

As you read, what did you notice about the influence of these different king's mothers and fathers? What type of an influence did your parents have upon your spirituality? What type of influence will you have on your children's spirituality?

If you were given only a few verses in scripture to describe your life, goals, desires, and righteousness, what do you hope would be written about you?

Day 219, 2 Kings 16:5-17:41

Ahaz formed a political alliance with the king of Assyria to protect Judah from Syria and Israel (2 Kings 16:5-9). When Ahaz visited Damascus, the capital of Syria, he found an idol altar. Watch for how Ahaz defiled the temple and abandoned true temple worship in favor of the popular approval of the king of Assyria in 2 Kings 16:9-20. In what ways are people tempted to abandon the worship of the temple of the popularity and praise of the world today?

In 2 Kings 17, you will learn about the lost ten tribes of Israel. Assyria conquered Israel and carried the inhabitants away as captives, thus they were scattered among many nations of the earth and were indeed lost. Look for some of the reasons the Lord allowed Israel to be destroyed in 2 Kings 17:1-23. Are people becoming lost today because of these same types of activities? What role have you played in the gathering of the lost tribes?

2 Kings 17:24-41 describes how the land of Israel was inhabited by people from other nations who struggled to live up to the Lord's standards. This group of people came to be called Samaritans. By the time of Christ, there would be centuries of hard feelings between them and the Jews.

Day 220, 2 Kings 18

So many of the kings we have studied have failed to do what they should, but not Hezekiah, king of Judah. He will not disappoint you much. Look for what he did in verses 1-8 in order to be different from the other kings you have studied. What did you learn about Hezekiah that will help inspire you to be different, so you can make a difference?

To mess with Assyria by not fully paying their demanded wages is to court death. Assyria invaded the land of Judah and wiped out small towns along their way to Jerusalem (:9-17). Assyrian armies were known for their unbelievable violence, but they also sent professional spokesmen, whose purpose was to cause trembling fear through psychological torment. Rab-shakeh was one of these men. Watch for all the diverse ways he sought to destroy the people's confidence in Hezekiah and to doubt God in verses 19-35. You may want to read this out loud to get the full impact of it.

Rab-shaken was terrifyingly persuasive, but notice how the people responded to him in verse 35. There are people like Rab-shaken who seek to destroy your confidence and faith in God. When should we be silent to those who mock our beliefs and faith, and when, or how, should we speak up?

Day 221, 2 Kings 19

With the Assyrian army camped outside the city of Jerusalem and Rab-shaken literally breathing out threatenings, Hezekiah was under some stress. Look what he did in verses 1-8 during these impossible situations. What impossible situations have you come through by following the same pattern?

Rab-shaken didn't want the people of Jerusalem or King Hezekiah to think this deliverance was a miracle from God in verses 9-13. Look for what Hezekiah did when Assyria returned in verse 14. When you find yourself in real trouble, do you take the time to spread the problem before God in prayer? What question, problem, or situation should you have been spreading before God?

Look for how verses 15-19 are a fitting example of a real prayer. Check out the Lord's answer and promises given through the prophet Isaiah in verses 20-34. Then note the miracle in verses 35-37.

Day 222, 2 Kings 20-21

In the midst of the Assyrian siege years, king Hezekiah became deathly sick. Look for the miracles that came because of Hezekiah's prayers in 2 Kings 20:1-11. What expected and unexpected miracles have you received as a result of real prayer? What miracles are you currently seeking through prayer?

In 2 Kings 20:11-21, you will see one of the few mistakes King Hezekiah made during his leadership. What evidence can you find in these verses that the mistake came because Hezekiah was not looking to or thinking about the future? How can looking to and thinking carefully about the future help you in your leadership and parenting?

I have wondered if this lack of looking to the future was one of the reasons why Hezekiah's son Manasseh "built up," "reared up," "made," "used," "dealt with," "set," and "seduced… [His people] to do more evil than did the nations whom the LORD destroyed before the children of Israel" (2 Kings 21:1-9). So much evil was done that the Lord declared He would wipe Jerusalem, as a man wipes off a dirty plate (2 Kings 21:13).

Manasseh's son Amon walked in the ways of his father (2 Kings 21:19-21). What kinds of personal commitments are you making to ensure that your children learn the gospel and practice living it?

Day 223, 2 Kings 22-23

Josiah was a righteous king, who sought to turn his people from idol worship by repairing the temple in 2 Kings 22:1-7. During the renovation, the scriptures were discovered in the temple. What happened next in 2 Kings 22:8-9:3 is an great story about how the word of God can change individuals and society. What happens to individuals and society when they don't have or heed the word of God? What happens to individuals and society when they have and heed the scriptures?

2 Kings 23:4-24 contains the magnificent work of idol destruction. When you study scriptures what types of things do you want to change about your life?

Because of the profound changes that happened to individuals and society, look in 2 Kings 23:25 for what was said of Josiah. Finish the following phrases:

"The scriptures influence me to …"

"Then, like King Josiah I can influence others to …"

Day 224, 2 Kings 24-25 and 1-2 Chronicles

It was most likely during the time of Josiah when someone made a set of scriptures out of brass plates so that they would never be lost again. Then, just 60 years later, Nephi would obtain these plates to build the faith of the Nephite and Lamanite nations. Just as the Nephite prophets were inspired to construct the gold plates, someone was inspired to create the brass plates. What an exciting story that will be one day. What will you do to make sure that the scriptures and the lessons they teach are available to others?

Following the reign of King Josiah, Kings Jehoahaz, Jehoiakim, Jehoiachin, and Zedekiah all did wickedly before the Lord. In 2 Kings 24:14-17 you will see several captives are taken to Babylon. This is where the book of Daniel begins (Daniel 1:1-4). In 2 Kings 24:18, Zedekiah was set up as a king. This is when the story of the Book of Mormon begins (1 Nephi 1:4). In 2 Kings 25:1-7, Jerusalem was captured and Zedekiah's eyes were put out. This is the beginning of the Mulekites, who will eventually meet up with the Nephites in the Promised Land (Omni 1:14-19). Where will your story and faith fit in the history of the world?

1-2 Chronicles is a fast-paced history of what we have covered so far this year. If you want, you can review what you have learned this year by reading through each chapter heading. What new details did you learn? What were you reminded of that you had forgotten?

Day 225, Ezra 1-3

Jerusalem was captured by Babylon in 587 B.C. The Persians overthrew Babylon in 539 B.C. Look for all the different people who were inspired and ways that were prepared in Ezra 1 so the Jews could return to rebuild the temple. What evidence did you find in this chapter that God will inspire members of other faiths to help with His work?

Ezra 2 list all the people who returned with Zerubbabel. This chapter is proof that regular people matter. One day, God will list all His children who will return home. Look for why some were not allowed to return in Ezra 2:61-62. Notice, in Ezra 2:69, how people contributed to the building of the temple. What is your ability to donate to, go to, or serve in the temple?

In Ezra 3:1-7, the temple altar was rededicated. Look for how the people responded when the foundation of the temple was laid in Ezra 3:11-13. What similarities did you see between this event and the dedication of a modern-day temple?

Day 226, Ezra 4-6

"We completed a temple in Kirtland and in Nauvoo, and did not the bells of hell toll all the time we were building them? They did, every week and every day" (Brigham Young. *Journal of Discourses* 8:356). Why does Satan fight so hard against temples? Look for all the means that were employed to stop the construction of the temple in Ezra 4.

From 530-520 B.C., the work on the temple ceased. Look for the determination and faith shown by the prophets Haggai, Zechariah, Zerubbabel, and others in Ezra 5. Which verse do you think describes this miracle better, 8 or 11? How do you think this same group would describe the temple building time in which we live?

In Ezra 6 Darius searched and found the original decree from Cyrus that allowed the Jews to continue and finish the work on the temple (:1-15). In verses 21-22, we learn that the temple and Passover/sacrament is to separate us from the world by turning us to seek the Lord and receive His joy and strength. How are you being separated and strengthened through your participation in sacred ordinances?

Day 227, Ezra 7-8

When there are problems on the earth, the Lord sends people with the needed gifts and talents to provide relief and help. Look for how Ezra was prepared to help with leading the second wave of Jews back to Jerusalem from Babylon in Ezra 7:1-10. Make sure you really spend some time with verse 10. What problems has the Lord sent you, with your gifts and talents, to heal? What additional preparation, learning, or skills might the Lord want you from you, in order to become the solution you were born to be?

What did Artaxerxes do to show his support of Ezra and the temple building project in Ezra 7:11-28?

Ezra received permission to lead a group back to Jerusalem with tremendous riches to help beautify the temple. Among the problems they faced was a trip of more than 900 miles through thief-infested land. Look for what the people were directed to do in Ezra 8:21-23. Then look for the result in verses 31-36. When have you utilized fasting to help you find solutions to your problems and concerns? Which problems currently puzzling you might be helped by fasting?

Day 228, Ezra 9-10

Have you ever made one of your parents or youth leaders do what Ezra did in Ezra 9:3-5? This is not an overreaction; look for what the people had done in Ezra 9:1-2. When we are heavy with the weight of others' choices, we should take these burdens, as Ezra did, to the one Being who can heft them. Look for the power of the honest and humble prayer offered in Ezra 9:6-15.

Note how Ezra helped the children of Israel repent from their sin in Ezra 10:1-17. In Ezra 10:18-44, a list was made of all of those who married outside of the covenant. Marriage is always an eternal choice and worth listing and noting. What will you do to make sure that you and your loved ones make the sacrifice and choices that will lead to temple marriages? What will you do to make your marriage an eternal one? What will you do to make sure that the blessings of a temple marriage will continue to be yours?

Day 229, Nehemiah 1-2

As you read chapter 1, look for how Nehemiah responded when he learned that Jerusalem and its people were in ruins. Have you ever felt such personal devastation because of the condition of others? Who is a person in your life for whom you often pray the way that Nehemiah prayed for Jerusalem (:5-11)?

What were the circumstances that led to Nehemiah gaining permission from King Artaxerxes to leave and rebuild the walls and gate of Jerusalem (Nehemiah 2:1-11)? What does this tell you about how the king must have viewed Nehemiah? Nehemiah was placed, by the Lord, in a strategic proximity to king Artaxerxes. Why have you been placed in your time and location? Who are you to influence? What mighty work does God have for you to do?

Before including others, Nehemiah first took time to think, survey, and prepare in Nehemiah 2:12-16. Before a leader can give vision and direction to others, he must have a plan, even if it costs him some sleep (:15). How did people react to Nehemiah's invitation in Nehemiah 2:17-20? Which side are you on when a prophet of God asks you to do something?

Day 230, Nehemiah 3-5

As you read Nehemiah 3, look for and mark the phrases "next unto Him" and "after him." No one ever builds the kingdom of God alone. This is a group effort. Someone has served before us, and someone will serve after us. Who are the people you admire that served before you? What are you doing to be sure there are people who will serve after you?

What opposition did they face as they built the wall, and how did they overcome it in Nehemiah 4? What lessons are in this chapter for those who face opposition as they seek to build the kingdom today?

Read the chapter heading to Nehemiah 5. Nehemiah's counsel to the rich rulers was: Don't burden the work of the Lord by trying to get rich off your brothers and sisters.

Day 231, Nehemiah 6-7

As members of the Church, we are engaged in a magnificent work. There will be many attempts made to stop or slow this work. What lessons can you learn from Nehemiah, in the sixth chapter, about how to avoid being deceived, slowed, or halted in your work? Try to come up with at least four principles.

You may also want to study President Dieter F. Uchtdorf's General Conference talk from April 2009 titled "We Are Doing a Great Work and Cannot Come Down."

Nehemiah 7 is the same story as Ezra chapter 2. You may want to read both chapter headings to refresh yourself on the content.

Day 232, Nehemiah 8-10

How many ways can you find in Nehemiah 8:1-9:3 where the people showed a remarkable amount of love and respect for the word of the law or scriptures? What do you do to demonstrate your love and respect for the word of God?

Nehemiah 9:4-35 is a great review of the whole Old Testament up to this point. Look for how often the attributes of God, like His graciousness, mercy, slowness to anger, and kindness, are mentioned.

Look in Nehemiah 9:36-38, the heading for Nehemiah 10, and Nehemiah 10:28-31, and 10:37-38 for what the people were willing to do once they had studied the scriptures and reviewed the stories from their past. How can studying scriptures increase a person's desire to make and keep additional commandments and covenants? Now that you have been studying scriptures, what is the next commandment or covenant that God would like you to seek to keep?

Day 233, Nehemiah 11-13

Chapter 11 contains a list of many who were selected to live in Jerusalem. We also learn that most were asked to live in neighboring cities (:1). Chapter 12 lists many of the priests and Levites who were called to serve in the temple. Every town has advantages and disadvantages to it. One of the great advantages is your ward and fellow church members. Rather than reading chapter 11-12, I invite you to look through your ward directory and consider ways in which you and those members have loved, served, learned, and grown together. What testimony could you share about the blessings of having a ward family?

How cool is the principle that God can turn a cursing into a blessing (Nehemiah 13:2)? When was the last time God manifested this power in your life?

Nehemiah left Jerusalem for a time. When he returned, he found corruption in the temple, breaking of the Sabbath day, and marriages made outside the covenant. Look for how the heartbroken Nehemiah reacted to each of these in verses 6-14, 15-22, and 23-31. In verses 14, 22, and 31 Nehemiah asked the Lord to remember him for the good he tried to do among these people. How will the Lord remember you: as one who tried to keep or break covenants and commandments?

Day 234, Esther

Esther is a long and complicated story for one day. You can read each of the chapter headings, watch one of the churches videos on Esther, or read the chapter in the *Old Testament Stories* reader. Once you know the story and can tell it in your own words, look up a few of the key passages.

- 1:1-19
- 3:8-13
- 4:1-17
- 5:1-14
- 6:6
- 7:10

What can chapter 1 teach us about the dangers of alcohol? What positions or places have you been placed in so that you can accomplish wonderful things? In what ways can you have your faith manifest itself in Christian courage today?

Day 235, Job 1

As you read verses 1-5, look for what kind of a man Job was. Then, look for what the Lord and Satan said about Job in verses 6-12. What did Satan want to do to test Job? This is a poetic narrative style of writing that emphasizes Satan's role as our adversary, so don't get too worked up about the interaction between God and Satan.

Look for what happened and how Job responded in verses 13-22. What did you find remarkable about how Job responded? How do you think you would have responded?

Day 236, Job 2

In verses 1-8, look for what Satan and God said about Job this time. What did Satan get permission to do to Job, and what did he not get permission to do? Why do you think it is important to know that there are always limits upon Satan?

Discover how Job's wife responded to his poor health in verse 9. In what ways is it tempting to blame God for things? Now, look in verse 10 for how Job continued to show his faith in God. How do you think your faith would be doing? What do you think your prayers would be like?

What can you learn about how to be a great friend from verses 11-13?

Day 237, Job 3

Look at the type of questions Job had for the Lord (:11). I have a quote that will forever ruin you when it comes to asking such questions, or, in other words, if you apply it, it will drastically bless your life. Do you want it?

> When you face adversity, you can be led to ask many questions. Some serve a useful purpose; others do not. To ask, why does this have to happen to me? Why do I have to suffer this, now? What have I done to cause this? will lead you into blind alleys. It really does no good to ask questions that reflect opposition to the will of God. Rather ask, what am I to do? What am I to learn from this experience? What am I to change? Whom am I to help? How can I remember my many blessings in times of trial? ...This life is an experience in profound trust—trust in Jesus Christ, trust in His teachings, trust in our capacity as led by the Holy Spirit to obey those teachings. ... To trust means to obey willingly without knowing the end from the beginning (see Prov. 3:5–7). To produce fruit, your trust in the Lord must be more powerful and enduring than your confidence in your own personal feelings and experience (Richard G. Scott. "Trust in the Lord," Ensign, Nov. 1995, 17).

What did you learn about questions you *could* ask versus questions you *should* ask?

Day 238, Job 4-37

These chapters are incredibly steep in poetry and thought as Job and his friends discussed several deep subjects and questions. We do not have the time and space to cover them adequately. As you read the chapter headings listed next to the following names, list some main thoughts or questions by each person. You can do this in two ways. First, you can read the chapter heading straight through and follow the back-and-forth discussion between the friends, or, second, you can look up each chapter heading to gain insights into the individual who is speaking.

- Eliphaz 3-4, 15, and 22
- Bildad 8, 18, and 25
- Zophar 11, and 20
- Job 6-7, 9-10, 12-14, 16-17, 19, 21, 23-24, and 25-31
- Elihu 32-37

Some of the best passages from these chapters are 5:17-27; 14:14; 19:23-27; 20:5; 23:1-17; and 32:8.

Day 239, Job 38-42

After all the friends of Job had their turn speaking, the voice of the Lord was heard. Look for and mark many of the questions that God asked Job to prove that He, the Lord, should be trusted. When we are experiencing troubling times, we often ask God questions that He isn't interested in answering—questions that don't seek revelation and action, but that arise from our doubtful hearts. We would do better to ask questions that demonstrate faith and trust in the Lord. We might still go farther and consider what questions God might have for us in those times to remind us why we, like Job, should trust Him. What questions might God have for you at this moment in your life?

The divine principle of compensation is promised to all those who endure well. Look for how the story of Job ends in chapter 42. Where can you find evidence that God consecrated Job's afflictions for his gain? What current struggle will God turn into a blessing one day?

Day 240, Psalms

In the Bible Dictionary, there is very interesting entry called "Quotations from the Old Testament in the New Testament." What did you notice about the amount of times the book of Psalms is quoted? Many of these quotations are prophecies about the Messiah that are fulfilled by the life of Jesus Christ. It was this discovery that finally endeared me to the book of Psalms. These quotations are listed below. Read as many as you would like.

- Psalms 2:1-2 is fulfilled in Acts 4:25-27.
- Psalms 2:7 is fulfilled in Acts 13:33.
- Psalms 2:9 is fulfilled in JST Rev 2:27.
- Psalms 16:9-10 is fulfilled in Acts 13:34-37.
- Psalms 22:1 is fulfilled in Matt 27:46.
- Psalms 22:7-8 is fulfilled in Matt 27:39, 43.
- Psalms 22:16 is fulfilled in John 20:24-27.
- Psalms 22:18 is fulfilled in Matt 27:35.
- Psalms 31:5 is fulfilled in Luke 23:46.
- Psalms 34:20 is fulfilled in John 19:31-33, 36.
- Psalms 41:9 is fulfilled in John 13:18, 21-27.

- Psalms 65:7 is fulfilled in Matt 8:26.
- Psalms 69:9 is fulfilled in John 2:14-17.
- Psalms 69:21 is fulfilled in Matt 27:43.
- Psalms 78:2 is fulfilled in Matt 13:35.
- Psalms 91:11-12 is fulfilled in Luke 4:10-11.
- Psalms 110:1 is fulfilled in Matt 22:41-46.
- Psalms 118:21-2 is fulfilled in 2Luke 20:17-19.
- Psalms 118:26 is fulfilled in Matt 21:9-11.

Why do you think the past prophets were given such a detailed account of the Savior's life? If ancient prophets gave prophecy about the Savior so that we wouldn't miss him, then what do you think is the role of the modern prophet?

Day 241, Psalms to Music

If you look up "Psalms" in the Bible Dictionary or in the "Guide to the Scriptures" at LDS.org, you will find that many of the songs were set to music. The book of Psalms is an ancient hymnbook. I am going to offer you three different challenges you can do for your study today. Each of these could become a separate project to continue your study.

- In the back of any LDS hymnbook—paper or digital—there is a section titled "Scriptures." Here you will find a list of scriptures, from the Old Testament through modern scripture, that are associated with the hymns. Psalms is the most used book of scripture for this list. You can study as many of these references as you would like.
- You could look up and study the hymns listed next to the scripture references from Psalms.
- You could look up a favorite hymn or two and study the text for important ideas and insights.

Day 242, Psalms the Top 10

The book of Psalms is so popular that it and Proverbs are often included in pocket editions of the New Testament. The wonderful thing about the book of Psalms is that you do not need to know the context of any verse in order to derive great meaning out of it. The bad thing about the book of Psalms is that you do not need to know the context of any verse in order to derive great meaning out of it. Therefore, it is usually used as a go-to, flip-the-book-open-and-point when someone has forgotten that they are supposed to share a scripture during a devotional. Please don't do this when it is your turn; come prepared.

Today however, we are going to embrace, but modernize, the flip-and-point method of finding a great scripture. I would like you to do a Google search for "Most popular verses in the book of Psalms." There will be lots of different website options—and it doesn't really matter where you go—but lists are nice for this type of activity. Read and ponder several of these verses and then make your own top 10 list from what you have read. You may want to make a list at the beginning of the book of Psalms. Now you don't ever have to flip and point again.

Day 243, Proverbs Knowledge, Learning, and Wisdom

The key theme in the book of Proverbs centers on knowledge, learning, and wisdom. Below are several of the key passages about this theme. After you read each one, record what it teaches you about knowledge, learning, or wisdom.

- Proverbs 1:5-7
- Proverbs 2:2, 6 and 10-11
- Proverbs 3:5-7
- Proverbs 3:11-12
- Proverbs 4:5-6
- Proverbs 8:10-11
- Proverbs 9:9-10
- Proverbs 12:1 and 15
- Proverbs 15:14, and 32
- Proverbs 17:27-28
- Proverbs 19:20
- Proverbs 22:6

What are you doing to increase in knowledge, learning, and wisdom? When was a time that you had to trust in the Lord, rather than in your own wisdom and logic (Proverbs 3:5-6)?

Day 244, Proverbs Themes

The book of Proverbs has several other major themes. Try to find a couple of verses for each of the following themes, and write them down. To help you find them, you may want to do a Google search for "Verses from Proverbs about _____." The verses you find may not all come from the book of Proverbs. You may have to sift through a list to find your picks.

- Communication
- Encouragement
- Faith
- Family
- Folly and foolishness
- Funny

For the final theme, you may need to change the wording of the search to something like "Funny verses from the book of Proverbs." Enjoy.

Day 245, Proverbs Themes Day Two

I hope you enjoyed the activity from yesterday because today we are going to continue to study a few more specific themes. So, get your Google glasses ready. Again, type in the phrase "Verses from Proverbs about _____", and remember to sift through the findings to locate the verses from Proverbs that you like on this topic.

- Happiness
- Lust
- Morality and ethics
- Relationships
- Work

Day 246, Proverbs PESTS

We always hear people say that the solutions to life's problems are in the scriptures. Today, we are going to learn a strategy for discovering some of our problems and then see if we can find some solutions in the scriptures. The word PEST is an acronym that stands for People, Environments, Situations, and Things. Next to each letter list all the things in that category that cause you stress, problems, worry, or anything else.

P

E

S

T

Now that you have identified some things that cause you problems, let's find some solutions in the book of Proverbs. Read anywhere you want—even skip around—for 10 minutes and see what answers you can find to your problems. You may want to write verses by the problem in your PEST chart. What does this teach us about scriptures? What does this teach us about Proverbs? What does this teach us about problems?

Day 247, Proverbs 31

What warnings are given to leaders or the popular in verses 1-9? How could you change these verses to be equally meaningful to women?

Verses 10-31 comprises one of the greatest salutes to virtuous women in the scriptures. As you read each of these qualities, think of the virtuous women in your life—one for each quality who has been a fitting example of living that principle.

What updates and modifications would you add to this list so that it shows love and gratitude toward those virtuous women in your life?

Dear sisters, daughters, mothers, grandmothers, wives, aunts, and women in general, thank you for all the unnamed and un-thanked tasks, services, and blessings you provide.

Day 248, Ecclesiastes 1

How might a person who has no understanding of the Plan of Salvation complete the following phrase? "The purpose of life is…"

The intent of the Preacher, assumed to be Solomon, is to answer such tough questions as those found in verse 3. To help with your understanding of this book, it is important to know definitions for two frequently used terms. The phrase "under the sun," means a worldly viewpoint. "Vanity," as used in this work, means temporary, fleeting, meaningless, and not satisfying. Read Ecclesiastes 1 and note how poorly the Preacher's first attempt at giving purpose to a life without a plan unfolds.

How are you currently feeling about the value of your daily thoughts, feelings, and actions?

Day 249, Ecclesiastes 2-3

If ever there was a person who had the ability, money, and time to find happiness in temporal possessions, it was King Solomon. Study Ecclesiastes 2 for all the numerous ways that Solomon tried to acquire satisfaction and happiness. What did he ultimately conclude is the value of these activities if a gospel purpose is removed? Ecclesiastes 3:14 explains how the works of God are eternal. Because we are eternal creations, our work and labor also become eternal in nature. What current activities and labor are providing you with happiness and eternal value?

Ecclesiastes 3 lists several different events that commonly occur in a person's life. What are some of the times and seasons of your life right now? What are some things for which there will be time one day? What are some things for which you will no longer have time one day? What are some of the essential things for which you will make time, regardless of the season of your life?

Day 250, Ecclesiastes 4-12

Read the following key verses and the chapter headings for each chapter and ponder on some interesting principles (4:1-3, 9-10; 5:2-3, 10-12; 7:1, 12, 20; 9:11-12, and 18). Which of those verses did you enjoy pondering?

We started studying Ecclesiastes with a question about how a person without a knowledge of the Plan of Salvation would view the purpose of life. Read Ecclesiastes 12:13-14 to discover the conclusion of the Preacher.

How would a person with a knowledge and understanding of the Plan of Salvation finish this statement? "The purpose of life is…"

Day 251, Song of Solomon

You have probably heard stories about people ripping out the pages of this book or stapling them shut. Before you do either of these options, look for what was said in footnote 1a by Joseph Smith about this book. Then, look up "Song of Solomon" in the Bible Dictionary and find out why some people are opposed to this book and why it is included in the Bible.

The best example of this allegoric love is found in chapter 3. Read verses 1-3 and look for evidence of this individual's commitment to seek out and find a lover. This is a fitting example of how we should seek for Christ.

Look for the commitment that the searcher declared when that lover was finally found in verse 4. Can you say the same thing about your relationship with Christ? What types of things try to loosen your grip on Him? Will you hold Him and not let go?

Day 252, Introduction to Isaiah

Let's dispense with the "I'm scared of Isaiah" stuff. I love Isaiah, and I'm excited for the experience you will have studying him. The Lord, Himself, has commanded us to read Isaiah (3 Nephi 23:1). Nephi read Isaiah to his brothers to persuade them to believe in Christ (1 Nephi 19:23). Nephi and Jacob quoted extensively from Isaiah, because like them, he had seen Christ in vision (2 Nephi 11:2-3). Isaiah speaks of Jesus Christ using 61 different names and titles. Isaiah is quoted 137 times in the New Testament. Make sure to look up "Quotations" in the Bible Dictionary to see the most significant ones. Eighteen of the 66 chapters are quoted in their entirety. Of the 1,289 verses in Isaiah, 433 are quoted in the Book of Mormon; that's 35%. Some of those are quoted repeatedly, raising the number to 600 total verses quoted in the Book of Mormon. Isaiah is mentioned 106 times in the Doctrine and Covenants, either quoting, referencing, or interpreting him. Isaiah was a prophet for 40 years and counseled four different kings from 740 B.C. to 700 B.C. Tradition states that King Manasseh put Isaiah in a hollowed tree and then had it sawn in half with him inside (Bible Dictionary p. 707). Isaiah's wife was a prophetess, who allowed her sons to become walking object lessons—their names serving as reminders of great lessons that they wanted people to remember (Isaiah 7:3, 8:3).

In 2 Nephi 25:1, it was mentioned that it helps to understand Isaiah if you understand the ways the Jews prophesied. Isaiah was a literary master. He nearly always wrote in a Hebrew poetry style called parallelism. This means he repeated himself on purpose, clarifying points by using different words to describe the same thing. This means that Isaiah only says half as much as you think he does as you read his words. It is this repeating of thought that often causes readers to be confused, we think he is moving on, when really, he is trying to make sure we understand his point. Check out these popular verses and watch for how he repeats himself in Isaiah 1:18; 5:20; 53:3-5; and 55:8-9. Could you see it? Because of this writing style, I have found Isaiah to be easier to understand if I look for the parallels and read the text out loud.

Isaiah also used dualistic symbols and prophecies. This means he used one symbol to talk about two different things, or even two separate times. The virgin birth, prophesied in Isaiah 7:14, was about Isaiah's wife having a baby and about Mary and Jesus Christ. The stump with a new branch growing out of it (Isaiah 11:1-12) was about Christ and Joseph Smith. Because of this dualistic nature, time also becomes problematic. Isaiah will be speaking about the Millennium and then shift to the Last Days, which is before the Millennium. Reading chapter headings and footnotes helps to orient yourself.

Isaiah was also a political, historical, and geographical genius. There are 106 various places named in this book, and Isaiah threw in all the names, symbols, traditions, and kings of these places. This often confuses readers because we are unfamiliar with all these names and their ambiguities. You don't have to look up all these names and places to understand Isaiah because he repeated himself, and he taught simple major truths about the gospel.

Look in 2 Nephi 25:1-8 for any final counsel that Nephi gave about how to understand and learn from Isaiah.

Day 253, Isaiah 1

Look in verses 1-9 to discover ways in which Israel had offended the Lord. According to verses 10-15, why did the people feel as if they didn't need to repent? What will you do to make sure that your meetings, ordinances, and sacrifices are worshipful and not just visual?

The Lord makes a number of promises to those who repent in verses 16-19 and 25-27. Which of these promises do you love?

Verses 20-24 and 28-31 relate what the Lord promises to those who will not repent.

Day 254, Isaiah 2

In verses 1-5 Isaiah saw people gathering to the temples in the last days. Look for the blessings that result from gathering to and attending the temple. Which of these blessings have you noticed in your life?

After mentioning several excellent blessings for attending the temple, Isaiah tells us about the things that keep people from being able to qualify for the blessings of the temple in verses 6-9.

Verses 10-22 speak of the Second Coming of Jesus Christ. Look for what will be brought down low or humbled, and what will be exalted and raised up in that day. What can you do to keep humble now so that you will not have to be humbled in the day of the Lord?

Day 255, Isaiah 3

This chapter is a splendid example of Isaiah's dualistic ability to make a prophecy apply to at least two different times. Verses 1-12 describe the results of wicked behavior upon both Isaiah's Kingdom of Judah, as well as modern Israel. Look for what happens to leadership and compassion when wickedness is selected over righteousness. Verse 8 points out that it is not only what we do that can be wicked and harmful, but also what we say.

In verses 13-15, the Lord declared that He will pass judgment for the mistreatment of the poor. One of the reasons people do not properly care for the poor is because of the ancient and modern obsession with fashion and style, leaving no resources for the poor (:16-24). In verses 16-24, look for how well Isaiah detailed the problem of being obsessed with fashion as well as the promised consequences for that obsession. What will you do to make sure that your style of dress doesn't diminish your donations and care for the poor and needy?

Day 256, Isaiah 4

Some have thought that verse 1 is a reference to polygamy being reinstated. The shortage of men in verse 1 is a result of the battle of Armageddon, mentioned in verses 25-26 in the previous chapter. This cannot be polygamy because the women fend for themselves and are not supported by the men.

Verses 2-6 deals with the women who survived the judgment of the last chapter. They will be called holy (:3) after they are washed (:4) and their righteous influence will be so great that every house will become like a temple (:5-6). What do these verses teach us about the impact that a righteous woman can have on the world?

Day 257, Isaiah 5

The song of the vineyard in verses 1-7 contains several wonderful analogies comparing how Lord treats the vineyard and how he treats the house of Israel. What evidence of justice and mercy did you see?

The term "woe," which is used seven times in the next few verses, is associated with the anguish and distress of those who receive the judgment of the Lord. Following is a summary of each:

- Verses 8-10 speaks out against the improper use of land.
- Verses 11-17 contains the prophetic word on the way those of the world improperly—and with evil intent—eat, drink, and make merry.
- Verses 18-19 is directed against those who are wicked and mock God and His divine plan.
- Verse 20 speaks against liars and those who fight against the things of God.
- Verse 21 deals with conceited individuals who believe themselves to be wise.
- Verses 22-23 accuses those who give bribes and belittle the righteous.

Which woes do you feel are in abundance in our world today?

Verses 25-30 describe how the Lord, in a wicked world, will reach out His hand to save all He can by raising up His ensign/church. He also calls to all nations by His missionary servants and the Holy Ghost to be gathered to safety. Why do you think it is important to know that the Lord continually seeks to reclaim those who are engaged in wicked practices?

Day 258, Isaiah 6

In verses 1-5, Isaiah saw the Lord and a number of six-winged angels, covering their feet and eyes. This angel's depiction is a complex symbol of imperfection. In Hebrew writing, the number seven is symbolic of perfection, thus an angel with six wings is not yet perfect. Additionally, feet are symbolic of actions and choices while eyes symbolize light and knowledge. Therefore, the covering of feet and eyes show that the angel did not walk a sinless life and still lacked light and knowledge. Still, this imperfect angel symbol highlights the goodness and perfection of God by proclaiming, "Holy, Holy, Holy." (:2-3). Following this vision, Isaiah felt unworthy because of sins that he committed with his mouth (:5). Of which un-repented sins would you be aware if you were to come into the presence of the Lord?

In verses 6-7, Isaiah's sins were forgiven as a hot coal was placed upon his mouth. The coal came from the altar, upon which sacrifices were offered;

thus, the coal represents the Atonement of Christ being laid upon Isaiah's sins. How have you experienced a purging of sin like Isaiah? Why is a searing hot coal a good symbol for repentance and forgiveness of the Atonement? Upon what things do you need to have the Atonement placed so that you can be clean and healed?

After being cleansed, Isaiah was ready and willing to accept a difficult call to be a prophet, which will result in few people being converted before his death (:8-13). How does experiencing the Atonement in our own lives help to make us willing and able to serve the Lord and others?

Day 259, Isaiah 7

This chapter contains an account of a time when the Kingdom of Judah was threatened by Syria and Israel. In verses 1-9, the Lord had the prophet Isaiah proclaim to Ahaz, the King of Judah, that Syria and Israel would be destroyed. For assurance of this prophecy, the Lord promised a sign of a virgin bearing a son (7:14). This is an example of a dualistic prophecy that was fulfilled twice: once, with the birth of Isaiah's son through his righteous and virtuous wife, and the second through Mary and Jesus Christ. The name *Immanuel* means "God with us" (:14e). Please ponder about times when you have felt that God was with you, not against you or for you, but with you.

In verses 17-25, Isaiah told of the coming invasion of Assyria against Judah. Notice the repeated phrase "in that day" and "in that same day" (:18 and 20-22). There are several footnotes to help with understanding verses 15-25.

Day 260, Isaiah 8

In verses 1-4, we see the first fulfillment of the prophecy made in yesterday's reading about a virgin bearing a son. The second will come with the birth of Christ. Isaiah and his wife, the prophetess, were to have a son, Maher-shalal-hash-baz. It was prophesied that before he was old enough to talk, Syria and Israel with their capitals—Damascus and Samaria—would be destroyed and they will no longer threaten the kingdom of Judah.

In verse 18, we learn that Isaiah's sons were to be signs to the people. Both of their names teach valuable lessons. Maher-shalal-hash-baz means destruction is imminent (:1d), and Shearjashub means a remnant shall return (Isaiah 7:3a). Thus, any time people met Isaiah's sons, they would know that the Babylonian destruction would one day come and that a remnant of those carried away would also return.

Verses 5-16 speak about how the people rejected trusting in Jehovah and instead put their trust in making alliances with the King of Assyria to deliver them from their problems with Israel and Syria. This rejection is described as the people rejecting the softly rolling waters of Shiloah, a little stream near the Temple Mount, for the great, but unpredictable and dangerous, Euphrates, a river in Assyria known for its flooding. After Assyria destroyed Judah's enemies, it turned on Judah and almost annihilated them. Why do you think people are prone to reject the soft but steady safety and counsel of Jesus Christ and seek other solutions?

In verses 17-22, we learn that our God is a master of hide and seek. Why do you think He stays hidden unless we look and then wait for Him? We could all take the advice that President Monson gave to a downcast and overwhelmed leader: "It is better to look up" (Carl B. Cook. "It Is Better to Look Up," Ensign, Nov 2011).

Day 261, Isaiah 9-10:4

Yesterday we learned that those who look to the earth or man for answers will receive darkness and dimness. Following the destruction of the kingdom of Israel by Assyria and the kingdom of Judah by Babylon, a long darkness dwelled upon the Promised Land, but Isaiah promised a day of light when he prophesied of Christ's coming (Isaiah 9:1-2).

In Isaiah 9:3-7, we find one of Isaiah's most well-known prophesies about the coming Messiah. What are the names that will be given to Him? These names are not just titles, but also calls to action. Consider the following questions for each name: How did he, how does he, and how will he fulfill each of these names and titles for us collectively and to you individually?

Isaiah 9:8-10:4 contains a warning of destruction to the northern ten tribes of Israel, as well as to modern day Israel for their wicked deeds described in Isaiah 9:14-17. Despite the rebellion and rejection of Christ, He still stands with "his hand stretched out still" to save or to destroy (Isaiah 9:12, 17, 21; 20:4). How will use your agency today to reach out for the salvation and help which Christ offers?

Day 262, Isaiah 10:5-34

In verses 5-11, the Lord said He used the Assyrian King and army to punish disobedient and wicked nations like ancient Israel had become. This whole idea can be summarized by looking at D&C 117:6.

After the Lord used Assyria to destroy Israel, He then destroyed Assyria like He will do with all wicked and filthy things at His coming (:12-19). Notice how the King of Assyria boasts of his perceived strength and power, like an axe in the hand of its master (:13-15). How will you boast of the Lord today rather than of yourself?

In verses 20-27, the Lord promised eventual deliverance to those whom Assyria destroyed if the people would return and "stay upon the Lord" (:20). Check out footnote 20b for a greater understanding of what it means to "stay upon the Lord." Also, notice how deliverance comes because of the "anointing" (:27). These verses remind me that weekly, hourly, and daily, I don't stay upon the Lord or His Atonement like I should. How will you depend upon the Lord today, even this hour?

After destroying the Northern Kingdom of Israel, Assyria then sought to march to Jerusalem in the Southern Kingdom of Judah. Verses 28-32 contain a list of cities that were destroyed by Assyria. Nob is only 1.5 miles from Jerusalem. The people and their king, Hezekiah, continued to stay upon the Lord with the enemy at their gate. The Lord then cut down Assyria like a tree and saved His people (:33-34, and 2 Kings 19:35). He will do a similar work at His Second Coming.

Day 263, Isaiah 11-12

Here are some cross-references that will be very helpful in studying Isaiah 11: D&C 113:1-6, JSH 1:40, and Revelations 5:5.

Assyria was cut down yesterday, typifying the destruction of the Second Coming. Nothing but stumps remained. Today, in Isaiah 11:1-9, we will see a description of how Christ's millennial reign will begin. Look for how He will rule and govern. Also look for the conditions that will exist during the Millennium.

The image of a new branch growing out of a cut stump continues to be used as Isaiah, now jumping from the Millennium back to the Restoration. The cut-down trees now represent the age of apostasy, and the newly restored Church and its leaders are the branch shooting forth (Isaiah 11:10-

16). What is taught in this section that helps you want to be faithful, and gather others to the ensign before the Savior's millennial reign?

As far as Isaiah 12 goes, we should thank Heavenly Father and Jesus for what they do, and praise them for the type of beings they are.

Day 264, Isaiah 13

Verses 1-5 speak of the Lord's army that has been gathered together to defeat the world, or land of wickedness. What do you think is the difference between a person who volunteered for this army, rather than someone who feels that they were drafted?

The destruction of the wicked is a sure promise, but it doesn't have to be a destruction of the people. It can be the destruction of wicked thoughts, feelings, and actions (:6-22). This whole chapter is a call for us to become a member of the Lord's hosts—one of His sanctified ones, His people (:3-4, 22). What blessings do you think await those who choose to fight this battle every day versus those who chose to fight when they were faced with physical destruction?

When Babylon was destroyed, it was completely wasted. Isaiah promised it would never be dwelt in or inhabited again (:20).

Day 265, Isaiah 14

Verses 1-11 deal with the rest and peace that came when the king of Babylon was no more. When this oppressor of Israel was gone, they could again gather to their homelands. This is also symbolic of the rest and gathering that will one day come to all.

Verses 12-23 are about the fall and destruction of Satan. Notice that he is called Lucifer in verse 12. This is a correct use of the name, for Isaiah is speaking of the pre-existence. Satan is no longer worthy of the name Lucifer; he lost it with the use of his agency. Look up the word "Lucifer" in the Bible Dictionary to learn more about what this means. This doesn't mean he was second in command or even the only other option; that idea is most likely a lie he wants us to believe. In today's section, the Lord, through his prophet Isaiah, will reveal the true intentions and desires of Lucifer in the premortal life. In verses 13-23, look for what Satan wanted and what he will receive. What attitudes led to Satan's ultimate demise? What will happen to us if we possess those same attitudes?

Over the past several chapters, Isaiah has been giving us a great contrast between the Savior and Satan with these prophecies and names. Satan wanted to be above God; he became jealous of Christ and was only thinking of himself. On the other hand, we have "with us is God" (Isaiah 7:14). Heavenly Father and Jesus Christ want nothing more than for us to be partakers with them of the divine.

Our Heavenly Father and His Son, Jesus Christ, are significantly beyond our comprehension in the perfection of their attributes and character, and yet all they do in their work and glory is seek to raise us up to their level. By contrast, Satan seeks to constantly push us down. Satan never wanted to be equals with God. He wanted to be viewed as better. Thus, in our day-to-day life, do we seek to lift and encourage others, or do we look for reasons to view ourselves as better?

Day 266, Isaiah 15-16

There are 16 cities from all over Moab named in Isaiah 15. Note the exhaustive nature of the destruction and devastation promised to Moab or the wicked. Do you think it is the Lord's or Isaiah's heart that was crying out for Moab in Isaiah 15:5 and 16:11? Either way, what does that teach about how the Lord and His prophets feel about the wicked and their punishment? Is there someone for whom your heart cries because of their choices?

Look at how graphically the need for a Savior is described in Isaiah 16:1-4. Verse 5 is a promise of that deliverance.

What sins led Moab to experience such devastating consequences, according to Isaiah 16:6? How do these sins cause devastation in your life?

Day 267, Isaiah 17

What is the purpose of before-and-after pictures? Look for all the before-and-after images used in verses 1-6 to describe Israel.

Note how Israel felt about themselves before the Assyrian destruction in verses 10-11. Then notice how they feel about themselves after they get through the humbling the Lord prepared for them in verses 7-8.

How do you think Israel felt about themselves before and after? How do you think God felt about Israel before and after? What do you think other nations thought of Israel before and after (:12-14)? What do you think God wants you to get from all of this before-and-after stuff?

Day 268, Isaiah 18

This chapter is about the three remarkable gatherings that will occur in the last days. The first gathering is to the ensign of truth raised by the restoration and proclaimed by the personal ambassadors of the Lord, His missionaries in verses 1-4. This gathered people will eventually become a gift to be presented to the Savior at His Second Coming (:7). What gifts, talents, time, and energy are you frequently submitting to this collective present?

The second gathering is of the wicked "sour grapes," or cut-off branches (:5). Why are spoiled, rotting fruit and cut branches an appropriate image for the wicked?

The third gathering is the horrific promise that, because of the destruction of the wicked before and after the Second Coming, the Lord will gather the fowls of the air and the beasts of the earth to devour the corpses (:6). This event is called the Supper of the Great God, and it is prophesied in multiple scriptures (D&C 29:17-20; Ezekiel 39:12, 17-20; Revelations 19:17-18; and JSM 1:27).

In what ways does our decision of whom we gather with now help to determine with whom we will be gathered later?

Day 269, Isaiah 19

God needed to help His disobedient children that inhabited Egypt. Because He is a remarkable parent, He planned to punish them in such a way that it would lead to healing. Look for how Egypt is smitten in verses 1-17. What afflictions has the Lord caused or allowed to happen to get your attention before? Notice in verse 2 how the destruction of a whole society began with the destruction of family relationships.

What did the Lord do to heal Egypt in verses 18-25? The use of the word "Lord" was sprinkled a few times throughout the verses speaking of punishment, letting us know of His involvement (:1-17). Now, consider marking, just how involved the "Lord" is with the healing process mentioned in verses 18-25.

Which has the Lord done more in your life: smite or heal? The answer to that question reveals more about you than it does the Lord.

Day 270, Isaiah 20-21

Take the time to draw a picture of what the Lord asked Isaiah to do in Isaiah 20:1-6. Hahaha! Why would the Lord ask His prophet to do such a thing (2a, and 5a)? This is a great chapter. How would you finish the following phrases?

- "God always has His prophets…"
- "Without the covering and protection of the atonement we are left…"
- "Oh Babylon, oh Babylon, we bid thee farewell. For we're going to heaven and you're going to…"

That last phrase goes with Isaiah 21. The prophet Isaiah saw and then proclaimed the destruction of Babylon 200 years before in happened (Isaiah 21:2b). This chapter and its footnotes are worth your time.

Day 271, Isaiah 22

When people know that war is coming, there are preparations to be made. Isaiah 22:7-11 lists some of the things the people did to be ready. Look in Isaiah 22:11-14 for what they should have done to get ready. How can following this same counsel help us as we prepare for education, missions, marriages, work, parenthood, and service?

Look for hints that show that Isaiah 22:15-19 is a warning to the proud.

Shebna was an example of those who look to themselves. The priest Eliakim's blessing in Isaiah 22:20-25 is an example of one who looked to his Maker. Eliakim's life was also a dual prophecy of the Savior. Look for all the prophetic parallels.

Day 272, Isaiah 23-24

Tyre was a large Phoenician city that was obsessed with merchandise (Isaiah 22:2-3 and 18). Do you have any shopping habits that may need to be refined or corrected?

The destruction is described in Isaiah 24:1-4, 6-13, and 16-23 as a desolation, a confusion, a leanness, a treacherous blow, a pit, and a prison. Read Isaiah 24:5 to discover what actions caused such a thorough desolation.

How do we avoid destruction, pits, and prisons? We must do the exact opposite of the things mentioned in Isaiah 24:5. How has the restoration of the gospel and the Church helped you to do these things?

Day 273, Isaiah 25-26

In the past several chapters, we have seen the promised destruction of several nations and lands who have refused to be obedient to the teachings and covenants of the Lord. As you study Isaiah 25:1-9, look for what the Lord says about those who hearken to His teachings and covenants. Nearly every line is significant. Which of those promises are you personally looking forward to?

The justice of God is great for the righteous and terrible for the wicked. As you read Isaiah 26:1-18, you will find references to both. Look in Isaiah 26:19-21 for the promises the Lord makes to His people. How can you tell if the Lord considers you to be one of His people? Look for the difference between Isaiah 26:8-9 and 10-11. What did you find?

Day 274, Isaiah 27-28

In Isaiah 27, the punishments and blessings of the Millennium continue. What will the Lord do in verses 1-6 to show His great care for His people? Where can you see missionary and temple work mentioned in verses 12-13? Performing temple ordinances one by one will take a long time and be a major effort during the Millennium. Why do you think it is important that those ordinances for the dead are done on an individual basis?

Look for the specific mode of teaching the Lord used in Isaiah 28:9-13. Why does this work so well? As people learn this way, why might they not see much progress in themselves at times?

Which of the terms used in Isaiah 28:16 do you like for the Savior? How has He been each of those for you?

How is Isaiah 28:20 a great description of what life is like without the Atonement?

God is a perfect farmer. He knows exactly what each plant needs to yield forth a fruitful crop. Watch how He treats each type of plant differently in Isaiah 28:23-29 to get the best out of them. What outstanding lessons did you learn about God, teaching, parenting, and farming from these verses? How hard does the Lord need to work you over to get your best results?

Day 275, Isaiah 29:1-12

Without the help of modern scripture and prophets, a person might think this chapter is just another prophecy about how Israel will be redeemed from destruction. A more expansive version of this chapter is found in 2 Nephi 27 in the Book of Mormon. The JST of verses 1-8 or 1a make it clear that these verses describe the apostate conditions that will exist in the world following the apostasy. In what ways is a dreaming and drunk man a good image for those living during the apostasy (:8-10)?

Verses 11-12 are a prophecy about an experience that occurred in Church history and can be found in JSH 1:63-65. Study the prophecy and then study how it was fulfilled. Later, Charles Anthon would deny that he had endorsed the note and claim that he counseled Martin Harris that Joseph Smith was a fraud. However, Martin went to New York with several personal doubts and when this experience was over, he was completely committed to the cause of publishing the Book of Mormon, even at the loss of some of his farm. The fulfillment of this prophecy increased the faith and commitment of Martin Harris, how about your faith and commitment?

Day 276, Isaiah 29:14-24

Yesterday we studied the conditions surrounding the coming forth of the Book of Mormon. Today, we are going to look at some of the problems that the Book of Mormon was commissioned to resolve. Let's begin with the location problem of hearts and lips in verse 13: Where are the hearts and lips, and where should they be? This problem was so prevalent that Jesus Christ quoted this verse to Joseph Smith during the First Vision (JSH 1:19). The Book of Mormon and the restoration of the gospel were designed to draw our hearts, and not just our lips, closer to God (:14). Have you felt this shift in your heart as you have studied the Book of Mormon?

What other problems and solutions did Isaiah say the Book of Mormon would handle in verses 15-24?

After reading these verses, how would you finish the following phrase? "If I study the Book of Mormon I can…"

Day 277, Isaiah 30

With the Assyrian empire approaching, the kingdom of Judah sought to make an alliance with Egypt. As you read verses 1-17, look for places where Judah refused to trust in their God and follow His prophets, and instead trusted in Egypt to save them. When troubling times arise in your life, what are the things you sometimes look to as "saviors" rather than the Lord? Note what these people wanted from their prophets in verses 9-11. When you hear a prophet speak, do you wish they would change or do you wish that you will? What change have you made lately, or what change will you make because of the words of a prophet?

For those who sit still and wait upon the Lord, the promises are immense, and some are mentioned in verses 18-26. I love verse 21. Which blessing and verse do you love?

What, you want more promised destruction? Okay, here it is: verses 27-33. Notice how the voice, breath, and language of the Lord is described. The Lord, as a righteous judge, has the right to have His words destroy. What about us; do we have that right?

Day 278, Isaiah 31-32

What are the people of Israel hoping will protect them, and what does the Lord say of these protections in Isaiah 31:1-3? What does the Lord say of His own protective powers in Isaiah 31:4-9? When were times in your life where you felt these protective powers wielded in your behalf?

Is there any current concern that you need to "turn" with to the Lord, so He can "defend," "deliver," and "preserve" you (Isaiah 31:5-6)?

When Jesus Christ begins His reign as King of Kings, many circumstances, traditions, and customs will change. What are some of these things mentioned in Isaiah 32:1-8? Your footnotes will be helpful with these verses.

Before the day of Christ's reign, many will be careless and at ease in their preparations for the destruction that is coupled to the Savior's coming (Isaiah 32:9-14). Isaiah 32:15-20 describes the feelings that the righteous will receive when the spirit of the Lord is poured out upon them and justice is poured out upon the wicked. Which phrase in Isaiah 32:17-18 articulates how the spirit often makes you feel?

Day 279, Isaiah 33

Verse 1 is for all those who think that the wicked don't get what they deserve. What ideas and attitudes do you like from the prayer of the saints in verses 2-6?

In verses 7-14, Isaiah again details the description of the wicked who will be destroyed. Then, in verse 14, the question is: Who can possibly escape this consuming destruction and dwell in the devastating glory of the Lord? The answer is in verse 15. What does it say we must be to escape the destruction that will accompany the glorious return of Christ to the earth?

The same glory which causes the fire that destroys the wicked is also the reward for the righteous—to be in the presence of "everlasting burning" (:14). Look in verses 16-24 for the encompassing blessings received by those who are worthy to stand in the Lord's glory. Would you be willing to change your speech, thoughts, and actions so that you can be comfortable in the presence of Christ when He comes again? How can weekly partaking of the sacrament help you accomplish this?

Day 280, Isaiah 34-35

As you read Isaiah 34:1-8, look for the staggering specificity of the Lord's wrathful judgment and the promised destruction. Verses 9-15 continue the destruction, with a horrific description of the devastation caused by the Second Coming, leaving places uninhabitable, except for the animals. With the earth cleansed of the wicked, the Lord then rewards those who have faithfully waited for Him with an everlasting inheritance of spouse and land in Isaiah 34:16-17. This is a wonderful reference to eternal marriage in the Old Testament. Why would heaven be incomplete if it was only about inheriting land or a place, but lacking the very thing that makes it a home: family?

There are several scriptures that state the Church was lost in the wilderness before the Restoration brought it back (D&C 5:14, D&C 49:24, D&C 86:3, and Revelations 12:1-6). Now that Zion has come forth out of the wilderness, or has been restored, look in Isaiah 35:1-10 for the abundant number of blessings and miracles to be poured out. Do any of those phrases parallel how you feel about building up the Lord's kingdom?

In Isaiah 35:8, we are told there will be a highway or a way to holiness revealed. How has the restored gospel helped you to get on the path to holiness? What does 2 Nephi 31:15-32:7 teach you about this path of holiness?

Day 281, Isaiah 36-41

Isaiah 36-39 cover the same material we covered in 2 Kings 18-20.

The events of Isaiah 40:1-11 are to be fulfilled twice. First, was through the mortal appearance of Jesus Christ with John the Baptist preparing the way (JST Luke 3:4-11). It will again be fulfilled when saints of the last days prepare people for Christ's coming and millennial reign (D&C 33:10). In Isaiah 40:12-25, there are 10 rhetorical questions asked to show the greatness of our God. What are the wonderful promises made in Isaiah 40:26-31 to those who wait, trust, and continue to believe in God? When was the last time you felt the fulfillment of those promises?

Isaiah 41:1-5 describes the Lord and what He has done. Then, in Isaiah 41:8-20, the Lord outlines a tremendous number of promised blessings to those who serve Him. As you read these verses, consider marking all those blessings you know you have received in one color, and all the blessings you are waiting to receive in a different color. Our God is kind. If you would like to know what God thinks about false gods, graven images, or our obsession with material gain, check out the Lords scathing language in Isaiah 41:21-29.

Day 282, Isaiah 42

This chapter contains a miraculous prophecy about the promised Messiah. What do verses 1-9 teach you about Jesus Christ and His mission as the Messiah? How incredible is the promise made in verse 3 and 3a?

Jesus will lead, straighten, and not forsake the blind who trust in Him, but those who trust in false gods will be ashamed (:16-17).

Because of their trust in idols, Israel was left blind, robbed, spoiled, snared, hid in prison, they had become prey, but the righteous will be honored (:18-25, 19a). Do you know anyone who fits into one of those descriptions? The solution to all those negative consequences is to be taken to the Messiah mentioned earlier.

Day 283, Isaiah 43

In verses 1-7, the Lord offers His paternal protection against water, fire, and other things. How might verses 1-7 help someone who is feeling discouraged?

In verses 8-13, we learn that the Lord expects us to be His witnesses to the world. What types of things could you witness or testify about God? God desires testimonies to be born of the things mentioned in verses 14-21.

In verses 22-28, it becomes clear that Israel wasn't praying or performing temple worship. The Lord wanted to forgive and redeem them, but Israel was weary of their God. He however was weary of their sin, but was still willing to justify and forgive them. If we are not careful, we could find ourselves repeating the past. What will you do today to remain grateful and repentant before God?

Day 284, Isaiah 44

The Lord declares that He is the only God in verses 6 and 8. What does He do in verses 1-8 as proof that He is the only God?

What does the Lord say in verses 9-20 about the absurdity of making and worshiping idols rather than your maker? What types of manmade objects do we worship in our day, even if no one prays to them?

What reasons does the Lord point out in verses 21-28 for why people should depend upon Him rather than their manufactured merchandise? Our God is not an egomaniac, so why does He plead for our repentance, our return, our restitution, and our worship?

Day 285, Isaiah 45

This chapter was written 200 years before Cyrus became the king of Persia. In what ways do verses 1-6 serve like a patriarchal blessing for Cyrus? What did the Lord do to help Cyrus know he was called by God to help the Jews return to their home land? What has the only true God sent you to this earth to accomplish?

What does the Lord say about His power and dominion in verses 7-25? What does the Lord say in those same verses to try to prevent the shame that those question Him and trust in idols will experience?

The idea that God is the only one and there is none else that can save is brought up several times (:5-6, 14, 21-22). How hard or easy has it been for the Lord to convince you of this truth?

What does verse 18 say about the why the earth was created?

Day 286, Isaiah 46

Isaiah 46:1-7 is a comparison between idols which must be carried about, versus God who has and can carry us. What troubles has God carried you through?

In Isaiah 46:5, and 9 God teaches that there is none that are like Him. As you read Isaiah 46:8-13 look for examples of God's exceptional power and ability. Do you think it would be acceptable to add the word "yet" to the end of Isaiah 46:9?

Day 287, Isaiah 47

Ancient Babylon's lifestyle was so rich and lavish in sin that Babylon has become a symbol for wickedness even now. Likewise, the destruction of ancient Babylon came so swiftly that it became symbolic of the destruction of the wicked at the Second Coming. What wicked beliefs and practices are listed in Isaiah 47:1-10 that provoked the destruction of ancient and modern Babylon? What will you do to provoke blessing from the Lord rather than curses today?

In the day when Babylon will be destroyed, what entities does the Lord invite Babylon to look to for deliverance, only to be disappointed in Isaiah 47:11-15? Is there anything you feel the Lord might add to update the list for our day?

Day 288, Isaiah 48

In verses 1-8, the Lord spoke to disobedient Israel. In what ways were they disobedient? To help Israel repent, what did the Lord allow to happen in verses 9-11? Despite Israel's wickedness, look for what blessings the Lord promises in verses 18-22 to those who repent, keep his commandments, and to the wicked, who do not. When does God send peace and when does He withhold it? How did obedience to the commandments bring peace to you recently? How has disobedience taken peace from you lately?

Day 289, Isaiah 49

In verses 1-13, the Lord promises His discouraged servants and people that He will gather them physically and spiritually. Before that time of gathering and healing many will have moments when they feel that God has forsaken them (:14). What does the Lord say about His ability to forsake or forget His people in verses 15-16? Why is this information vital to remember when we feel forsaken and forgotten by the Lord?

The Lord promises that He will gather His people and use the Gentiles in the last days to help nurse and lift those who return (:22-23). Who do you feel are the people that the Savior would have you nurse and comfort at this time? With some of these, you may feel that their redemption is impossible, like an prey caught by a lion. What does the Lord say about His power to redeem those who appear unredeemable in verses 23-26? When have you seen this miracle? Who do you hope and pray it will happen to next?

Day 290, Isaiah 50

Think of all the several reasons that are given for a marriage to end in divorce. Christ, on the other hand, is viciously committed to His covenant relationships. What do verses 1-3 say about Christ's commitment to us and His power to redeem us?

Mark the things that impress you about how Christ performed His mission to redeem us in verses 4-9. In what ways does Christ's commitment to fulfill His covenant motivate you to fulfill yours?

Because Christ fulfilled His covenant and mission, each person has two options before them: They can escape darkness and trust in the light provided by the Savior and the prophets (:10), or they can walk by the light of their own sparks (:11). When have your own kindled sparks proven futile when compared to the light of the Lord?

Day 291, Isaiah 51

Look for what the Lord says in verses 1-8 to those who are really trying to be righteous but get discouraged.

Why do people use alarm clocks? Israel wants God to awaken and show His strength like He did anciently to save them (:9-10). The Lord indicated that it is His people who need to awake, and to stop being afraid of men (:11-23). In verses 12-16, the Lord states that He is the same God that parted the sea, and hid them in the shadow of His hand. In what ways is God awakening to help us conditional upon our awaking from our sins and fears?

Day 292, Isaiah 52

Look for what the Lord invited Israel to do to awake from their spiritual sleep in verses 1-2. Check out D&C 113:7-10 for the Q&A session that Elias Higbee had with the Lord about these verses. What does verse 3 say about what we get for our sins and how we are redeemed from them? From which thoughts, feelings, or actions do you think the Lord would like you to awake and shake off?

Anciently, during times of war, people would anxiously await news from the battlefield. This news would have been brought by runners, traveling on foot. How do you think these messengers were received when they brought news that the battle had been won and peace was established? Look for how those who share the message of salvation are described in verses 7-8. Verses 9-10 shows the reaction of those who receive this message. What tools or methods are available today to help us proclaim the gospel to others? What successes have you had with any of these?

The message in verses 11-12 is for both those who are of Israel and those who are not.

Day 293, Isaiah 53

Every verse contains awesome prophecies about the Savior, His ministry, and His Atonement. Does verse 2 change the way that you view the Savior? In verses 3-6, notice what Christ does for us and what we do to Him. How could it have pleased Heavenly Father to bruise His son (:10)? What do you think it means when it says Jesus will "see his seed..." "...when he makes an offering for sin" (:10)?

With deep significance in every phrase, which idea about the Savior in Isaiah 53 did the Holy Ghost help you feel of its importance or understand more clearly?

Day 294, Isaiah 54

As you read this chapter, look for how Isaiah compares the sorrow, loneliness, and heartbreak of being scattered and then shows the promises of redemption. The Lord's covenant people will be compared to a tent, a barren woman, and a forsaken wife. All of Israel's deficiencies will be made up through the kindness of their Lord. Read these verses slow; read them out loud; and pray that you will feel the power of their truthfulness.

Look for what verses 1-3 say about the growth that Zion will experience someday.

In verse 10, what does the Lord through Isaiah promise will depart and be removed before His covenant and kindness? Do you feel this commitment from the Lord toward you?

There are forces in this world who seek to destroy faith in God, Jesus Christ, His prophets, and His Church. What do verses 15-17 say about such efforts?

Day 295, Isaiah 55

What is the Lord's sweet sales pitch and guarantee in verses 1-4 and 12-13?

Such a highly valuable treasure as the gospel does come with a price. Look for what payment the Lord demands for His blessings in verses 6-7. What would you say to someone who is hesitant about paying such a price?

How many concerns and problems could be solved if people remembered and believed the truths taught in verses 8-9? Is there some issue in your life that you need to approach and think about it like the Lord would?

Lucky for us, the Lord desires to teach us how He thinks. Search for the promise that the Lord makes about His words in verses 10-11.

Day 296, Isaiah 56

People at times may feel unwelcomed, and be treated as though they have no worth or potential. To all who have ever felt such things, look in verses 1-8 for the astonishing promises that the Lord makes to the stranger, the eunuch, the outcast, and to everyone who seeks to do God's will and honor the Sabbath. How is it possible for a covenant-keeper to receive a name better than family (:5)? How will someone who keeps his or her covenants become more than simply a son or daughter of God?

I've thought a lot about this and this is the best way to start my thoughts Some people are awesome, and some are not. If we are God's children, then what should we grow up to become? So why don't some people become awesome like God? Read verses 10-12, and look for the things that keep people from becoming awesome. If all I ever desire is food, drink, sleep, and entertainment, I'll never accomplish anything that is eternally significant. Why is the above statement true or false? Why shouldn't food, drink, sleep, and entertainment be the only things we desire? What else should we desire then?

Day 297, Isaiah 57

What are some of the reasons you have heard to justify adultery? Verses 1-13 outline Israel's unfaithfulness on their God.

Look for the promises that are given in verses 13-19 to those who have fidelity to God. Then, look for what is promised to those who are unfaithful in their fidelity to God in verses 20-21. Do the unfaithful gain any advantage over those who prove their faithfulness and fidelity?

How is your faithfulness and fidelity towards God?

Day 298, Isaiah 58

This is the best place in all of scripture to learn about the blessings of fasting, and the Sabbath day. Look for what the people of Israel should not have been doing in verses 1-5. Then look for the proper purposes behind why a person should participate in fasting in verses 6-7. What brilliant blessings are promised in verses 8-12 for fasting this way?

How does fasting increase your ability to live a righteous life? What are we trying to teach our bodies and our spirits by making them fast? What difference would it make if someone was trying to stop smoking, swearing, looking at pornography, or even eating unhealthily if he or she lived the law of fasting? What advice would you give to someone on how to fast and not just be hungry?

You may want to mark the wonderful promises for observing the Sabbath day in verses 13-14. How does the word "thine" in these verses help you understand what the Lord wants on the Sabbath? If a person understands this, why don't they need a list of what they can or can't do on the Sabbath?

Day 299, Isaiah 59

Take a moment to draw a pit with a man stuck in the bottom. In verses 2-15, Isaiah puts forth a vivid description of the sins that place us helplessly in a pit. What phrases, in these verses, best explains the condition of sin?

Seeing that there was no way for us to escape the pit on our own, the Savior enters the scene in verses 16-19 as our intercessor. Add the Savior to your drawing, standing on the ground above the pit. What do verses 1 and 20 teach us about what has to happen for the rescue to take place? What evidence has there been in your life that the Savior is offering you His hand and help?

To help us understand how committed the Lord is to His redeeming message, look in verse 21 for how long He wants it remembered and preached.

Day 300, Isaiah 60-61

Isaiah 60 is about Zion, the New Jerusalem. As you read this chapter, look for all the exceptional blessings and miracles the people will perform and enjoy because they chose to gather together in faith. Verses 17-22 seem to be obtained during the Millennium and also in the Celestial Kingdom. Which of those future lifestyle changes do you desire the most?

Isaiah 61:1-2 is so significant that when Jesus Christ read and declared these verses fulfilled to a group of Jews, they sought to kill Him (Luke 4:16-30). What does Isaiah 61:1-3 say about what Jesus Christ was sent to accomplish? Which of those mission statements have you accomplished in your own life?

The Lord has never forgotten His first love, Israel. As you read Isaiah 61:4-11, look for the blessings that the Lord will give to Israel when they return to Him. These are the same blessings that the Lord makes available to all His returning followers who have wandered off the gospel path. In what ways has the Lord been kind to you when you have strayed and returned?

Day 301, 62-63:14

In Isaiah 62:1, the Lord says he won't stop speaking or rest until Zion is blessed. Look in verses 1-5 for what blessings the Lord works endlessly to bring about. Then, in verses 6-7, we learn that the Lord has also set up watchmen or prophets, who will not stop working or speaking until the covenant people are the praise of the world and receive the blessings of verses 8-12. How does it make you feel to know that God and His prophets never cease seeking for ways to bless you?

In Isaiah 63:1-2, we learn that the Savior will wear read clothing during His Second Coming. As you study verses 3-14, look for ways in which red symbolizes both the mercy and justice of God. Footnote 2a also has several helpful scriptures. Will the Lord's display of color be a sign of His mercy or justice to you? In what ways are the justice and the mercy of God displays of His kindness?

Day 302, Isaiah 63:15-64:12

These verses contain a heartfelt prayer from the prophet Isaiah as he pleaded with God to bring the Second Coming. Take the time to read this prayer out loud, almost like you are the one offering the prayer.

What did Isaiah want God to do? What did Isaiah admit about our sins? Do you desire the Second Coming to come quickly, or do you long for more time to sin and repent?

What difference do heartfelt, ponderous prayers make in what you feel when you pray? Will you take the time to ponder as you pray today?

Day 303, Isaiah 65-66

Look for all the assorted reasons why the Lord could not manifest His power and glory to ancient Israel in Isaiah 65:1-7. Is there anything in your life that causes the Lord to hold back a display of His power in your life? Watch for how the Lord had to hold back blessings from those who refused to be His servants in Isaiah 65:8-16. Isaiah 65:17-25 showcases the brilliance of the millennial lifestyle that awaits those that faithfully endure.

People may build temples and offer sacrifices, but more than these the Lord greatly desires people to have broken heart and follow His way rather than their own (Isaiah 66:1-7). Zion will develop and be established as a nation, like a woman giving birth (Isaiah 66:8-14). When the Lord appears in His glory He will destroy with fire and judgment the wicked (Isaiah 66:14-18). What does 1 Nephi 22:16-17 say about why the Lord chooses to destroy the wicked? In the Millennium, a great amount of missionary work and shepherding people to the blessings of the temple will take place (Isaiah 66:19-24). Which message do you think Isaiah shares more, the destruction of the wicked or the blessing of the righteous?

Day 304, Jeremiah 1-2

As you read Jeremiah 1:1-5, look for when Jeremiah first received his call to be a prophet. We know this doctrine applies to all men and women who have received a calling from God to serve and teach others (Joseph Smith. *Teachings*, 365). Carefully and prayerfully complete the following sentence: "I believe God placed me upon the earth at this time to accomplish…"

What reasons did Jeremiah give for why he would not make an appropriate choice as a prophet in Jeremiah 1:6? What did the Lord say to Jeremiah in verses 7-10 and 17-19 to boost his confidence that he could accomplish what was being asked of him? What weakness of yours has the Lord touched to make it sufficiently strong to accomplish the tasks placed upon you (:9)?

In Jeremiah 2, the Lord outlines several reasons and examples of how the children of Israel have rejected Him. The message of this whole chapter can be boiled down to verse 13. How would you summarize, in our own words, which two sins the people were guilty of? What are you doing to make sure you are not guilty of those two sins?

Day 305, Jeremiah 3-6

In Jeremiah 3:6, 8, 11-12, 14, 22; and 5:6 look for a repeated word that describes the sinful struggle the Lord had with Israel and Judah. Why is that a perfect word to describe their—and, at times, our—sinful behavior? What are the sins that you continue to return to? Is the frequency of these sins increasing or decreasing?

Regardless of our sins and their repetition, look for what the Lord promised both ancient and modern Israel that He would do if they would return to Him in Jeremiah 3:12-19, 22, and 4:1-2. Have you felt the power of that promise when you have returned to God after sinning?

In Jeremiah 5:1, the Lord told Jeremiah that if he could find one just man, Jerusalem would be pardoned. This was an impossible task because of what the people had become. In the following verses, you will find an immense description of their sins. See Jeremiah 4:14, 18, and 22; Jeremiah 5:3, 7-14, 18-19, and 23-31; Jerimiah 6:7, 10, and 13-17. Did you see habits, traditions, and ideas that are also found in our society?

Day 306, Jeremiah 7-8

Jeremiah was commanded to stand at the gate of the temple and tell a special message to every person entering to perform ordinances (Jeremiah 7:1-2). Read Jeremiah 7:3-7, and look for what the people needed to amend or change about their behavior for them, the city, and the temple to be able to dwell forever through eternity. This chapter is a sobering warning to those who often attend the temple and partake of the sacrament. In Jeremiah 7:16, the prophet is told to "pray not" for these people. Look in Jeremiah 7:8-15 and 21-22 for how the people passed through the temple and offered sacrifices without allowing these ordinances to change and amend them. During your next appearance before the altars of the temple or sacrament table, will you ponder what amendments God wants you to make?

In the hymn "Did You Think To Pray," there is a line that says, "When your soul was full of sorrow / Balm of Gilead did you borrow" (#140). A balm is a gum or spice used for the healing of wounds. The area of Gilead was known for an abundance of plants that could be used for the making of balms (Bible Dictionary, "Balm"). Jeremiah 8:22 asks if there is no physician or balm in Gilead to help recover the people of Israel. While there is an ultimate physician and balm of healing in the Savior and His Atonement, the people of Jeremiah's day would not seek or use it (Jeremiah 8:20). Note the attitude of the people toward repentance, judgment, the word of the Lord, and shame in Jeremiah 8:5-9 and 12. Does your attitude toward these teachings allow for the balm of the Atonement to be applied generously to your wounds and problems? Do you have a problem or struggle right now for which you have pleaded for help?

Day 307, Jeremiah 9-15

These are some depressing chapters to study. To summarize, Jeremiah cried over the people's wickedness, and God told him not to pray for them because destruction will come. Here are some key verses for each chapter that will allow you to see the people's sins, God's glory, promised destruction, and great language.

- 9:2-7 and 23-24
- 10:10-13, 21, and 24
- 11:1-10, 18, and 20
- 12:1-3
- 13:1-11

- 14:10-12
- 15:15-21

Day 308, Jeremiah 16

What weird commandment did Jeremiah receive from the Lord in verse 2? I know, right? Those are kind of important things in the gospel. To understand why Jeremiah received such a command, look at verses 3-9.

In verse 10, look for the three questions the people of Israel have for the Lord. In verses 11-13, He gives His reply.

After Israel was scattered and driven because of their wickedness, look what the Lord promised He would do for them in verses 14-21. In what ways will the gathering of Israel in the last days be a greater event than the Exodus from Egypt led by Moses (:14-15)? Think of how many more miracles, missionaries, people, and years it will take. What do you think is the difference between a hunter and a fisher in this missionary metaphor? Why are both important? What lesson can you learn from the words "send," "many," and "every" in verse 16? The message is clear, even to those hidden in rocks, the Lord, through His servants, will find you. What is your story of the Lord finding and gathering you? What is your story of becoming a hunter or fisher for the Lord?

Day 309, Jeremiah 17

Verses 1-4, like many places in Jeremiah and in the Old Testament, speak about the deplorable false worship practices in which the children of Israel participated. These false worship sessions were often accompanied with the breaking of the law of chastity before an idol in a grove on the high places. No wonder the Lord's anger burned hot against them.

Verses 5-13 are wonderful verses about how those who trust in the Lord are blessed, while those who trust in flesh will be cursed. What images did Jeremiah use to convey these ideas?

If you were the Lord and your people were participating in false sex-based worship, wouldn't you have your prophet stand at every gate and teach the law of chastity? I would, but the Lord is so much more brilliant. Look for which lesson the Lord asks Jeremiah to teach at every gate in verses 19-24 and 27. Why would the Lord have Jeremiah teach that rather than the law of chastity? How could the consistent teaching and living of this gospel doctrine result in the eternal life and exaltation of everyone and the city (:25)? What does that teach you about the power of this teaching? Are you obeying this teaching in a significant way, so that the promises of verses 25-26 will also be yours?

If they will go to church and honor the Sabbath day by walking in the light, then they will be able to overcome and repent of their dark deeds.

Day 310, Jeremiah 18-20

In Jeremiah 18:1-11, the Lord had the prophet watch a potter create a pot that was marred and then recreate it. What was the lesson the Lord wanted Jeremiah to share with the people? Why do you think people fight the Lord so hard when all He wants to do is help, heal, and repair them? In the rest of the chapter, the people make plans against Jeremiah and he prays against them.

In Jeremiah 19, the Lord had the prophet get a pot and break it in front of the leaders of the people as a sign of unrepairable destruction that was to come. Is there something in your life that the Lord wants to help, heal, or repair that you are not allowing Him to?

In chapter 20, Jeremiah was put into stocks and, upon his release, continues to boldly prophesy the destruction of the Jerusalem by Babylon (:1-6). In verses 7-9, Jeremiah described his mistreatment and discouragement. He even wanted to stop speaking for and of the Lord altogether. What does verse 9 say about why he could not stop preaching? How bright does the flame of your faith burn when you face discouraging times in the service of your God?

Day 311, Jeremiah 21-22

King Zedekiah sent messages to Jeremiah to ask if the Lord would fight for Israel like in the ancient days. How did the Lord respond in Jeremiah 21:5-7, 10, and 13-14?

What do you think it would it feel like to know that God is against you?

In chapter 22, Jeremiah went down to the King of Judah to deliver his message of repentance or destruction (:3-5). Verse 8 points out that these people will be destroyed because they forsake their covenants. For example, Jeremiah compared King Josiah to three successive kings. Look for the difference between Josiah and Shallum/Jehoahaz in verses 11-17. Verses

18-23 are against Jehoiakim while verse 21 is a great description of how he responded to the Lord. Verses 24-30 are against Coniah/Jehoiachin; he was a useless pot and vessel (:28).

Day 312, Jeremiah 23

The Lord will drive and scatter the flock of Israel that the leaders failed to feed and protect (:1-2). Look for how verses 3-4 speak of the restoration of the Church. Then in verses 5-8, identify elements of the Savior's Millennial reign.

The Lord now begins to outline the sins of the spiritual leaders that caused all the people to error. What made these spiritual leaders—these professed prophets—such a menace, according to verses 9-32? Look what would have happened if they were what they were supposed to be in verse 22. What does verse 23 mean, and when have you felt this recently? How about verse 29?

Mark the word "burden" in verses 33-40. Why do you think the people used the word "burden" to describe the commandments and words of the Lord through His prophet? What truths were these people misunderstanding about God, His words, and His commandments? What word or phrase would you hope the people would use in place of "burden"?

Day 313, Jeremiah 24-25

In Jeremiah 24, the Lord reveals a vison about two baskets of figs. As you read this chapter look for what the Lord, and Jeremiah say about each of these baskets of figs. What kind of fig does the Lord think you are?

In Jeremiah 25:1-7, you will discover how a typical day of preaching went for Jeremiah. Why do you think it is important that Jeremiah rose early in the day (Jeremiah 25:3-4)? Jeremiah 25:8-11 describes the destruction of Jerusalem. Verse 10 lists things the Lord will take away from the people. What wonderful things have you lost before because of bad choices? Jeremiah 25:12-13 speaks of the destruction of Babylon. Jeremiah 25:14-38 is filled with promises of destruction to all kings and nations, "for the Lord hath controversy with the nations." (Jeremiah 25:31). What is the difference in your life when you are in harmony with the Lord rather than in controversy?

Day 314, Jeremiah 26-27

Jeremiah 26 is a wonderful chapter to read because of all the dialogue back and forth. In Jeremiah 26:1-7, the Lord gave instructions to Jeremiah and the prophet faithfully delivered the message. In verse 2, the Lord told Jeremiah to "diminish not a word." Why might a prophet, at times, want to diminish the words the Lord gives him? So, why don't they? Verses 8-11 contain the people's response to Jeremiah's preaching. Then in verses 12-15 Jeremiah responded to the people. The people then reacted to the words of Jeremiah and used the stories of Micah and Urijah to support their choice. How do you respond when the prophets ask you to change or repent?

What did the Lord have Jeremiah wear and send to the kings of many nations as a prophecy that Babylon would rule them in Jeremiah 27:1-11? Why might the words and prophecy of Jeremiah to King Zedekiah in Jeremiah 27:12-22 have been unpopular? What true, but unpopular, messages are the Lord's prophets delivering in our time?

Day 315, Jeremiah 28-29

In Jeremiah 28:1-4, Hananiah made a false prophecy about Babylon. Jeremiah responded by teaching people how to identify a true prophet by the teachings of verse 9. Hananiah then broke the wooden yoke that the Lord told Jeremiah to wear to symbolize the captivity of the Jews (Jeremiah 27:2). Look in Jeremiah 28:12-17 for how the Lord responded to the antics of Hananiah.

In chapter 29, Jeremiah made a true prophecy about the Jews' deliverance from Babylonian captivity. What counsel was given to these captive Jews about how to live in verses 1-10? What parts of that counsel would also be helpful to us as we approach where we live and callings that we get? Look at the promises the Lord made to the captive Jews in Babylon in verses 11-15. Then in verses 16-32, the Lord made some dire promises to the Jews still at Jerusalem.

Day 316, Jeremiah 30

What did the Lord have Jeremiah write about what the Lord would eventually do for His beaten, broken, and wounded people?

What physical, spiritual, mental, and emotional wounds has the Savior healed for you? What physical, spiritual, mental, and emotional wounds do you have that you know the Savior will heal?

Day 317, Jeremiah 31

Look for and mark power phrases that show the Lord's love, commitment, and eventual redemption for his people Israel.

What was your favorite phrase? Do you feel that the Lord could also use that phrase with you?

Day 318, Jeremiah 32

In verses 1-5, look for the reasons that King Zedekiah put Jeremiah in prison. While in prison, the Lord had Jeremiah purchase a field from his uncle's son (:6-16). Then in verses 17-25, Jeremiah recounted God's extraordinary abilities and asked God why He had him buy a field. What was God's symbolic purpose in having Jeremiah buy this field in verses 26-44?

What gestures and actions does the Lord have you do to symbolically remind you that He desires your salvation? According to 1 Peter 1:18-19, what did the Savior purchase as a symbol of His love and commitment to us?

What challenging thing will you do with the help of the Lord (:17, 27)?

Day 319, Jeremiah 33

As you search verses 1-14, look for what the Lord promises He will do for Judah and Israel. Don't you love the contrasts presented in verses 10-14? When have you witnessed the power of God to completely transform a person or a situation? What voices has God caused to be heard in your life that were previously absent (:11)?

Verses 14-26 end this communication of comfort with a divine prophecy about a Christ as the descendent of David.

Day 320, Jeremiah 34-35

In Jeremiah 34, King Zedekiah was rebuked in verses 1-7. Then, the king and his people momentarily tried to repent by allowing their slaves to go free, but they changed their minds and brought the slaves back into servitude in verses 8-11. Because of this half-hearted repentance, God pronounced that the king and his people would fall into the servitude of

Babylon in verses 12-22. What can this chapter teach us about mediocre repentance?

In contrast to the faithlessness in chapter 34, the Rechabites were completely committed to the principles taught by their father Jonadab to not drink wine or build houses (Jeremiah 35:1-11). Though the events in Jeremiah happened years before those in chapter 34, they were placed beside each other to show the Rechabites were strictly obedient to their physical father's teachings, while Judah rejected the counsel of their God (Jeremiah 35:12-19). Does this story increase your desire to keep the commandments and counsel of God?

Day 321, Jeremiah 36-39

As you read Jeremiah 36, look for how each person or group treated the sacred writings from God through Jeremiah. What can this story teach you about how to treat sacred writings?

What do chapters 37-38 teach us about how to treat the Lord's prophets? How did the people respond when the prophet told them things that they didn't want to hear? How do you respond when the prophets say things that are difficult for you to hear or receive?

Jeremiah 39 is the destruction of Jerusalem as a result of prophecies unheeded, scriptures tortured, and prophets imprisoned and ignored.

Day 322, Jeremiah 40-42

As you read chapter 40, note how well the invading and conquering forces of Babylon treated Jeremiah. There is a potential to treat the prophets worse if we don't hearken to them than if we just didn't believe them.

For chapter 41, just read the heading—unless you want to read of Ishmael's brutality; then read the chapter.

Fearing Babylonian recompense for the death of Gedaliah, the surviving Jews approached Jeremiah and asked for his advice and swore that they would obey in Jeremiah 42:1-6. Look at how long it took before Jeremiah got his answer in Jeremiah 42:7. What lesson can we learn from this? Look in Jeremiah 42:8-12 and then in verses 13-22 for the options that the Lord laid before the people. Which would you pick: Will you stay with the Lord and His promises to build and plant you, or do the logical thing and flee to Egypt for your lives (Jeremiah 42:7)?

Day 323, Jeremiah 43-44

In chapter 42, the Lord told the people not to flee to Egypt. In chapter 43 the people disregarded the counsel that came through the prophet Jeremiah and fled for Egypt, taking with them the prophet (Jeremiah 43:1-7). No doubt, we think of these people as foolish. Yet, is there some commandment, counsel, or quite whispering that you are currently disregarding?

How many ways can you tell people they will be destroyed? Let's find in Jeremiah 44. Look up each of the following verses for what is said about their demise (:6, 7-8, 11-12, 14, 22, 26, 28-30).

Day 324, Jeremiah 45-52

In the following chapters, Jeremiah made several proclamations of destruction against other nations. Look for what words, phrases, and images were used to describe their destruction.

- 43:4
- 45:4
- 46:5, 10, 11, 21
- 47:2-3
- 48:5, 8, 11, 12, 15, 17, 25-26, 31-33, 37, 38, 42-43
- 49:2, 5, 9-10, 12, 13, 15-17, 32-33, 37
- 50:2, 6, 10, 12, 13, 14, 22-25, 35-37
- 51:2

Another repeated theme that I love in these chapters is how often it is confirmed that the word of the Lord is coming to and through the prophet Jeremiah (42:7; 43:1; 44:1, 24; 45:1; 46:1-2, 13; 47:1; 50:1). Why is it comforting to know that the word of the Lord comes to a prophet?

Day 325, Lamentations 1-2

In Lamentations 1:1-11, the prophet Jeremiah presented his case for why he was lamenting or sorrowing for Jerusalem being destroyed by Babylon. Pick your favorite phrase that you feel best explained why Jeremiah was lamenting.

In Lamentations 1:12-22, the lamenting is now presented from the view point of Judah. How well do these verses describe the last time you also felt ashamed of your behavior before the Lord?

The language in Lamentations 2:1-9 and 17 is clear. The Lord made no excesses and claimed full responsibility for the destruction brought forth upon Jerusalem. The Lord is not afraid of His justice. He would rather have given mercy, but it was rejected. While the Lord was open about His involvement in the destruction, the children of Israel were destroyed because they refused to be responsible for their sins. How well do you claim responsibility for your actions?

Day 326, Lamentations 3-5

During his lament and mourning, Jeremiah stopped just long enough to build a chance of hope in Lamentations 3:20-33. What lines in this small section allow enough room for hope to exist even in complete destruction?

Lamentations 4 starts like chapter 1 by asking "how" questions? These questions might be written in the following manner. How did their faith fail? How did they fail to repent when so many prophets came unto them? How have those who were chosen to do remarkable things, chosen destruction instead?

Throughout Lamentations 4-5, the prophet continued to morn and sorrow for his city and nation. As you read these heartrending words, who are the individuals that cause you to mourn and lament? The book of Lamentations is proof of God's justice and destruction. But, if people repent, the principles of mercy and restoration will appear in there stead.

Day 327, Ezekiel 1

Look up "Ezekiel" in the Bible Dictionary. Determine what you can learn about the man and the book.

In Babylon, by the river Chebar, Ezekiel had a vision (:1-3). He saw beasts, wheels, and other crazy stuff in verses 4-25. If you will do a Google search for "Ezekiel's wheel" and then select image, you will find several artists who have attempted to capture what Ezekiel saw. In verses 26-28, Ezekiel saw the throne of God and fell on his face. Joseph Smith said, "Whenever God gives a vision of an image, or beast, or figure of any kind, He always holds Himself responsible to give a revelation or interpretation of the meaning thereof, otherwise we are not responsible or accountable for our belief in it.

Don't be afraid of being damned for not knowing the meaning of a vision or figure, if God has not given a revelation or interpretation of the subject" (Teachings of the Prophet Joseph Smith, p. 291). Even if we do not fully understand the meaning of what Ezekiel saw, his dramatic description can still give us a feeling for the incredible nature of the vision was and the greatness of God's glory.

Day 328, Ezekiel 2-3

In Ezekiel 2:1-3:14, Ezekiel received a call from God to preach the gospel. Look for what kind of people Ezekiel was called to preach to. What advice did God give to Ezekiel about how to preach to this group of people? In the middle of being called on a mission, Ezekiel was asked to eat a roll of scripture until he is full (Ezekiel 2:8-3:3). This eating of the scriptures is a symbolic representation about how we are to prepare before we teach and preach the gospel. You must first consume the word of God before you can teach it (D&C 11:21). Will you consume and devour the gospel the next time you must teach a lesson or give a talk? Don't you dare stand up and expect the Spirit of the Lord to help you if you have not feasted.

For seven days, Ezekiel sat, reflected, and pondered upon what had happened (Ezekiel 3:15). At the end of this time, the word of the Lord came again to Ezekiel. Look for what the Lord taught Ezekiel about the responsibility of being a watchman/prophet in Ezekiel 3:16-21. With their elevated view, what warnings and complements would the watchmen of today give to you at this point in your life?

Day 329, Ezekiel 4-39

As we read in the Bible Dictionary, the book of Ezekiel is divided up into three sections. Chapters 1-24 contain prophecies of judgment. Chapters 25-39 are prophecies of restoration. Chapters 40-48 are visions of the reconstruction of the temple. In chapters 6-39 Ezekiel uses the phrase "Know that I am the Lord" sixty four times (6:7,10,13,14; 7:4,9,27; 11:10,12; 12:15,16,20; 13:9,14,21,23; 14:8; 15:7; 16:62; 20:12,20,26,38,42,44; 22:16; 23:49; 24:24, 27; 25:5,7,11,17; 26:6; 28:22,23,24,26; 29:6,9,16,21; 30:8,19,25,26; 32:15; 33:29; 34:27,30; 35:4,9,12,15; 36:11,23,38; 37:6,13; 38:23; 39:6,7,22,28).

Reading and marking just a few of the above-mentioned scriptures will help make the message of these chapters clear: All the judgment, destruction, restoration, and rebuilding that God does, He does so that we might know that He is Lord.

What has He done during your life to help you learn this lesson?

Day 330, Ezekiel 11ish, and 18

Ezekiel 11:16-21 is a wonderful summary of the scattering and gathering of Israel. Ezekiel 11:5 is a verse worth marking.

Ezekiel 18:1-3 contain a popular proverb in Israel, saying if a father eats sour grapes it puckers the son's lips. What does God declare about judgment and how to be just in verse 4-9?

Ezekiel 18:10-13 speak of judgments upon the child of a righteous parents that becomes wicked, and verses 14-18 speak of the judgments upon the child who becomes righteous despite their wicked parents. What are some examples of both situations in the scriptures and from the lives of people you know? The principles that God really wants us to learn from these examples can be found in verses 19-20.

What does God say in Ezekiel 18:21-30 will be mentioned and will not be mentioned to those who turn away from wickedness to righteousness, and to those who turn from righteousness to wickedness?

To have the heart that God wants you to have, what are the things from which you feel God would have you turn away, and what are the things that He would have you turn toward (Ezekiel 18:31-32)?

Day 331, Ezekiel 33

Prophets were already compared to watchmen upon the towers in Ezekiel chapter 3. In Ezekiel 33:1-10 prophets and leaders are compared to watchmen. Look for the responsibilities and accountability for holding such a position. What happens to them if they don't do their calling well? What are some reasons why some leaders would not warn the people that they had stewardship over about their dangerous or damaging behavior? There is a danger if leaders only warn and correct others because they are worried about themselves, and not out of love and concern for those being corrected. Are any of the people for whom you have responsibility in need of warning or correction? If you will ponder and pray over them, God will provide thoughts and feelings about how you can warn them and correct them in a way that is best for both.

Do you think judgment of God is about the total amount of righteous actions and sins, or is it about direction? Search verse 11 for what God wants us to know about Him. In verses 12-13, what does God say about the righteous who turn to wickedness? What does God say about the wicked who turn to righteousness in verses 14-16? Some people think God's judgment is not fair (:17-20). Why do you think it is important to understand how Christ will judge us?

In verses 21-33, Ezekiel warned the people, and they listened to him, but they would not do what he said. Verses 30-32 are worth reading and marking.

Day 332, Ezekiel 34

I have never been able to forget the story told by President James E. Faust in the April 1995 Priesthood Session of General Conference about his lamb Nigh. The story is toward the front of the talk, or you can watch it from minute 3:36-7:30.

We will continue to learn about what shepherds or leaders should or should not do by studying Ezekiel 34:1-16. Hasn't Ezekiel been a wonderful book to learn about the responsibilities of being a leader? God and His prophet will not let this main idea alone.

Look for the special promises the Good Shepherd makes to His flock and people in Ezekiel 34:17-31. To whom does the Lord want you to be a better shepherd? How will you be a better shepherd to them? When has someone shepherded you like the Savior would have?

Day 333, Ezekiel 35-36

In chapter 35, God, through Ezekiel, promised perpetual blood, destruction, and desolation to the world of wickedness (see D&C 1:36 and "Idumea" in the Bible Dictionary). This chapter will put the fear into you and make you want to repent.

In Ezekiel 36:1-15, we get a notable prophecy and promise from God through Ezekiel toward the mountains of Israel. That's right, the mountains of Israel. It is almost as if God was apologizing for the wickedness they had to endure, and promises them relief and restitution. It will humble you to read it.

Ezekiel 36:16-23 is a reminder that Israel was scattered because of wickedness. Even among heathen nations—people without God—Israel would not repent but continued to profane God's name and covenants. Despite this long-standing wickedness, look for what the Lord will do for His covenant people in Ezekiel 36:24-38. What did the Lord say about His ability to change hearts and cleanliness? Why is it important not just to know this, but to also believe that Christ can change hearts? When have you seen Christ change a heart? What change of heart do you need Christ to give to you?

Day 334, Ezekiel 37

You are going to lose your mind when you find out just how amazing this chapter is. To prove that He would restore the children of Israel back to their Promised Land and covenants, God showed Ezekiel two miraculous events of things coming together that seemed impossible. The first was a vision of old, dry bones being resurrected, and the second was a prophecy of the Bible and Book of Mormon joining together.

There are not many people who were shown the Resurrection in vision and then wrote about it. What do verses 1-11 and 9a teach us about the Resurrection? Are you amazed or a little scared? I love these verses. When these members of the House of Israel are resurrected, God will tell them that He brought their bones together, and brought them out of their graves so that they could inherit their Promised Land (:12-14).

The next sign that God will restore Israel is the coming together of the Bible and the Book of Mormon in verses 15-20. To help you identify what is going on in the wording of these verses, check out footnote 16a; 1 Nephi 13:40; 2 Nephi 3:12; 2 Nephi 29:6-9,10-13; and D&C 27:5. Then Ezekiel 37:21-28 contains language like 2 Nephi 30 about how the children of Israel and the Jews will be physically gathered to their Promised Land so that they might be spiritually gathered and restored to their faith through the Book of Mormon in the Millennium.

These are extraordinary lengthens that God is willing to go so His people may know that He keeps His promises. Do you believe yet that God will keep His promises that He has made with you?

Day 335, Ezekiel 38-48

Ezekiel chapters 38-39 can be summed up by reading the chapter headings and looking up "Gog" and the scriptures listed in the Bible Dictionary.

In chapter 40-48, Ezekiel was taken up into a transcendent state, where an angel showed him a purified and rebuilt temple in Jerusalem. In Ezekiel 43:1-44:4, the glory of the Lord came and filled the temple. In Ezekiel 44:5-9, the prophet received pointed instruction regarding who can enter the temple and perform ordinances therein. Verse 9 mentions that people must be of the covenant by both their desires and works. According to Ezekiel 44:23, what is a major teaching that we are supposed to learn from the temple? How many ways does the modern temple teaches this same lesson?

Ezekiel 47:1-12 is a vision of a river of water flowing out from the temple, increasing in depth and providing miraculous growth and healing to everything it touches. As you read these verses, look for which of these symbolic blessings accurately describes the blessings that you have received from the temple.

Day 336, Daniel 1

In verse 1-4, look for what King Nebuchadnezzar had carried away when Babylon conquered Jerusalem. Verse 4 gives the qualifications of the young people that were taken. Would you have been in danger of being carried away?

The story in verses 5-21 is wonderful. In what way did these young people display great courage and commitment? Do you think this story is common or uncommon in the world today? What does this story teach you about friendship?

What blessings did Daniel and his friends receive for keeping a law of health in verses 15-21? How do those blessings compare with what is promised in D&C 89:18-21? Which blessings do you notice most from keeping the Word of Wisdom: the spiritual, mental, or physical blessings?

Day 337, Daniel 2

Search verses 1-16 for what happened to King Nebuchadnezzar, what he demanded of his wise men, and what Daniel did to help.

In verses 17-28, note what Daniel said about God and His attributes and powers. Which of the truths that Daniel shared about God impressed you? Why do you think it is important that Daniel magnified God's abilities rather than his own?

In verses 29-49, Daniel revealed both the dream and the interpretation of the dream. The king saw a great image with the different body parts made of various materials. This image represented several of the major kingdoms of the world. The golden head represented King Nebuchadnezzar and the reign of Babylon (:32 and 38). The chest and arms of silver represented Cyrus and the reign of Persia (:32 and 39). The belly and thighs of brass represented Philip and Alexander the Great of Greece (:32 and 39). The legs of iron represented the Creaser and the Roman Empire (:33 and 40). The feet and toes of mixed iron and clay represented various countries and European nations (:33 and 41-43).

There were only two images in the king's dream: the image representing the power and kingdom of men and the stone, which represents the restored kingdom of God (D&C 65:2). Daniel identified the timetable of this dream in verse 28 as taking place in the last days. Look for and mark the specific things that this dream teaches about the restored kingdom of God in verses 34-35 and 44-45. Which of those prophesies do you also know and believe? In what ways has the kingdom replaced the glitter and glam of worldliness in your life?

Day 338, Daniel 3

Whether King Nebuchadnezzar understood the dream, and realized that his rule and the reign of mortal men was limited, or if he misunderstood the dream and still needed to learn the lesson that the God of Israel is more powerful than the power of men, he still built a massive golden image and demanded that all people should worship it or be put to death.

As you study and ponder this remarkable story, consider what it teaches you about the importance of friends. Does the Savior fit in with your group of friends like He did here? We live in a world where it is hard not to let the environment of wickedness influence us. These three friends show us that we can live clean in any circumstance and not even get a smell of smoke upon us (:27).

Not even the mighty men that threw the three friends into the furnace could escape its heat. How does this story teach us what Shadrach, Meshach, and Abednego already knew about God—that He can deliver us out of impossible situations and problems (:15-18, and 29)? Out of which fiery furnaces has God delivered you in your life? Are there any fiery furnaces from which you are hoping and praying for deliverance right now?

When the Savior comes again we know that His brightness and glory will destroy the wicked (D&C 5:19). Look at this whole story. What do the actions and beliefs of Shadrach, Meshach, and Abednego teach you about how to be ready to abide the Second Coming and be worthy to stand in His presence and glory when others will not?

The king almost ruined the relationship he had with three loyal servants because of his rage and temper (:13, and 19). Does your rage and fury ever endanger the relationships that matter most to you?

Day 339, Daniel 4

King Nebuchadnezzar, not unlike many of us, was unwilling to put the lessons of the last few chapters to heart. Again, God granted unto the king a dream with significant meaning. The dream is found in verses 10-17. After reading the dream, but before reading Daniel's interpretation of it, offer your own thoughts on the meaning of the dream.

Now that you have made your own prediction, read Daniel's inspired interpretation in verses 17-27. Notice Daniel's concluding counsel to the king in verse 27 after revealing the interpretation.

The fulfillment of the king's dream and the significant lessons that the king and we are to learn are found in verses 28-37. What lesson has God tried at various times to teach you?

Day 340, Daniel 5

After the reign of King Nebuchadnezzar, his son Belshazzar began to rule. As you read verses 1-9, discover the mistake of the king and the miraculous event it created. Are there sacred things with which God would have you be more careful?

In verses 10-16, look for what spiritual gifts and talents people recognized in Daniel. Which gift do you think is most needed in our day? If others were going to identify your contribution to the kingdom of God, what gifts and abilities would they identify?

In verses 17-21, Daniel reviewed the lessons that Belshazzar should have learned from his father's life. In verse 22-24, Daniel identified the sins and mistakes of the king. Then, in verses 24-28, Daniel gave the interpretation of the writing on the wall. I love verse 27. What message do you think the Lord would write on your home or bedroom wall?

Day 341, Daniel 6

In verses 1-3, Daniel became an important figure to a third king, in two different nations. Why might some of the other councilmen have become jealous of Daniel? When others are blessed or praised do you sometimes get the utterly ridiculous idea that you don't matter as much?

Search verses 4-15 for the plan that the other leaders came up with to destroy Daniel. How do you feel about people who are able to make the right decision in difficult circumstances (:10)?

In verses 14-28, look for what King Darius did to try to deliver Daniel, and then what God did to deliver Daniel. What does this story teach us about the powerlessness of mankind, even mighty ones, and the power of God? Are there things in your life that you have no power to control, that you need to turn over to the great God of deliverance?

In what ways can the story of Daniel in the lion's den also be a symbolic teaching of Jesus Christ?

Day 342, Daniel 7-12?

Daniel chapters 7 through 12 contain an apocalyptic telling of the history of the world and the Second Coming of Christ. There is much of it—including specific details—that we don't understand, even though the meaning is clear. The world and its beastly desires will have power over the saints until the coming of the Son of God. The book of Daniel concludes with this revelation being sealed up, and the Lord not even giving an explanation to Daniel, His dream-interpreting prophet (12:4, and 8-9).

What we do know from modern prophetic commentary is that Daniel 7:9-14 is about Adam, the "Ancient of days," leading the great meeting to be held in Adam-ondi-Ahman. Here, all priesthood keys will be returned to Jesus Christ who will rule as Lord of Lords and King of Kings (Daniel 7:14, and 27). D&C 27 describes and lists many of the prophets that will turn their keys over during this sacred sacrament meeting or meetings. What does D&C 27:14-18 teach about what you must do to be worthy of such a united dispensational event?

Day 343, Hosea

Search Hosea 1:1-3, looking for who the identity of the husband and wife who are central to this story. What type of a woman was she? Now read Hosea 2:1-7 to see what happened next. If you were Hosea, how would you be feeling?

Rather than responding with anger and leaving her, note what Hosea did in Hosea 2:14-17 and 19-23. It is time to talk about the symbolism in this story. Hosea represents Christ and Gomer represents the children of Israel. What do you feel the Lord is trying to teach us so far in this story? In what ways is idolatry like adultery? In Hosea 2:5, we saw reasons that Gomer was unfaithful. What are some reasons you can pinpoint why people would ever be unfaithful to God?

Somehow Gomer got into so much trouble that she was sold into slavery. Look what her husband did for her in Hosea 3:1-3. How is this like what the Lord does for us?

This is a great love story because it shows us the power and commitment that God has toward His covenants. Search these verses and find one that helps you feel how much the Savior loves you: 2:14-15, 2:19-20, 2:23, 3:2-3, 6:6, 13:14, and 14:1-9. What has this story taught you about being in a covenant relationship with the Lord?

Day 344, Joel 1:1-2:10

Joel's message in today's section is universal to all people who are unprepared for the day of the Lord's judgment. The language is not trying to describe any specific event, but to create a sense of woe and warning to those who are living a life contrary to the will of God. As you study, look for which phrases matched how you felt when you were at odds with what the Lord had asked you to do.

In the Book of Mormon, the prophet Enos said he used strong and harsh language because nothing else would stir them up to repentance (Enos 1:23). Does God need to use strong language with you to get you to change and repent, or does it only take a quiet and gentle nudging through the Holy Ghost to prompt you to repentance?

Day 345, Joel 2:11-3:21

After promising destruction through harsh words in yesterday's reading, the Lord offers a chance to repent. What are the things the Lord wants people to do as part of their repentance in Joel 2:12-18 and 13b? If people will repent, the Lord promises to remove and reverse the punishments that were promised (Joel 2:19-27). The Lord also promises that the people will not be ashamed, and that they will be able to say God "hath dealt wondrously with" them (Joel 2:26). Has God dealt wondrously with you in removing your shame as you have repented?

When the angel Moroni appeared to Joseph Smith, he quoted Joel 2:28-32 and said it was about to be fulfilled (JSH 1:41). As you read Joel 2:28-32, look for the good and dreadful things that were to happen in the last days. Which of these promises have you personally witnessed or experienced?

In Joel 3:1-16, the nations of the earth are told that the Lord will "recompense upon" their "own head" destruction in the day of judgment and decision. While the world feels the roar and shaking of the Lord, "the Lord will be the hope of his people, and the strength of the children of Israel" (Joel 3:15-16). If you look and pray for it, the Lord will provide strength and hope for you today. Joel ends with the promise that, after the Lord's coming, He will dwell in Jerusalem and Zion (Joel 3:17).

Day 346, Amos 1-5

Amos was a pastoral prophet who prophesied the destruction of many cities because of a variety of sins in chapters 1-2. Look for the cities and the sins in Amos 1:3, 6, 9, 11, 13; 2:1, 4, 6-8, and 12. It's no wonder the prophet described his feelings as he did in Amos 2:13.

In Amos chapter 3, verses 3-8, the prophet asked several questions, which would be obvious to the people. If these things were obvious, then it was also obvious that before God does anything, He reveals it to His prophets (Amos 3:7). Amos then informed the people of their coming destruction in verses 11-15. Amos 3:7 ties God to His prophets in such a way that you don't get one without the other. What secrets of God have you learned through His prophets?

In Amos 4, we learn a fantastic truth about punishments and consequences. In verses 6-12, note how God afflicted this people and why. Did you find the repeated phrase? What punishments and consequences has God brought down upon your head to help you repent?

In Amos 5, the Lord, through His prophet, encouraged the people to seek Him, rather than sins, so they might live (Amos 5:4-8, and 11-14). If the people didn't seek God, they would find the day of His coming or judgment to be terrible (Amos 5:18-20). Finally, in Amos 5:21-26, God rejected the peoples' feasts and sacrifices because the Lord desires inward righteousness, and not outward displays of religion. How might people slip into that same mistake today?

Day 347, Amos 6-9

Amos chapter 6 begins with this sobering declaration: "Woe to them that are at ease in Zion." The whole chapter is a declaration that luxury can be detrimental. What are some of the dangers that may come from living in a world where we have tremendous wealth and possession?

In Amos 7:10-17, you will read about a marvelous interaction between Amos and Amaziah. What did you learn about Amos' call to be a prophet and how he responded to God and to others?

In Amos chapter 8, we learn that one of the major reasons the Northern Kingdom of Israel was destroyed was because of how they treated the poor (Amos 8:1-10). Amid these declarations of destruction, Amos described the state of apostasy in Amos 8:11-12. Why is that a perfect description of apostasy? What happens to people when there is no food or water? What happens to people when there is no word of God? Was there ever a time that there was a famine of the word of God in your life? Who do you know that is in the middle of a spiritual famine and drought?

Amos chapter 9 details the thoroughness of God scattering Israel and His promise that, in the last day, He will gather them together again.

Day 348, Obadiah

This is the shortest book in the Old Testament, and hardly anything is known of the writer. The name "Obadiah" means "servant of the Lord," so it could be a title. In the brief 21 verses that make up this book, the coming destruction of the Edom is foretold. The Edomites were the descendants of Esau, the brother of Jacob. Thus, the people of Edom were blood relatives of the Israelites. The promised destruction is a result of, first, Edom's pride (:3-9), and second, their participation and rejoicing in the destruction of Jerusalem (:10-16). These judgments teach us that pride, jockeying for position, and rejoicing over our siblings' struggles in a family setting are all displeasing to the Lord.

What can you do to continue to encourage and strengthen your family? How can this warning to Edom provide instruction to parents about things they should teach their family to avoid? What have you done, or will do, to develop an attitude of family love and cheerleading among your children?

Verses 17-21 speak of the redemption of Israel. Verse 21 mentions saviors on mount Zion. While Edom sought to destroy the family, Modern Israel seeks to redeem the family by providing the necessary saving ordinances in the temple that deceased ancestors could not obtain for themselves. How have you felt as you have followed the Savior's example by seeking to save the family of God through the performance of temple ordinances?

Day 349, Jonah 1-2

The book of Jonah has many principles that can change our lives. Here are some questions to draw those principles out.

- Why do we try to hide from what the Lord has asked us to do (1:1-3, and 10)?
- In what ways did Jonah's choices cause problems for others?
- Can geographical changes solve our problems?
- What does Matthew 12:38-41 add to our understanding of this story?
- What does Jonah 2:4-7 teach you about the power of the temple?
- Why do you think the fish spit Jonah up on dry land instead of in the middle of the sea (Jonah 2:10)?
- In what ways did Jonah experience the justice and mercy of God?

Day 350, Jonah 3-4

How did Jonah respond to the Lord, and how did Nineveh respond to Jonah in Jonah 3:1-9?

Look for how the Lord and Jonah responded to the repentance of the people of Nineveh in Jonah 3:10-4:1. Jonah's feelings are explained in Jonah 4:2-3, and 2b.

Jonah forgot the Lord's mercy that was shown to him in the belly of Hell. Look for what the Lord did and the questions He asked to try to help Jonah have compassion and mercy for others in Jonah 4:4-11. When has the Lord shown you forgiveness and mercy like He showed to Jonah and Nineveh? What has the Lord done to help teach you to have compassion and mercy on others? For whom does God want you to have compassion and mercy?

Notice that this story ends with a question. How Jonah chose to answer that question and how we choose to answer it determines more about ourselves than it does Nineveh and others.

Day 351, Micah 1-4

Which of these do you think we have spent more time studying about this year: doom and gloom or hope? What is the value of having the prophets talk about both? Micah lived in a time of wickedness in both the Northern and Southern kingdoms and was a contemporary of Isaiah and Hosea. In chapters 1-3, Micah promised destruction to Samaria, the capital of Israel, and Jerusalem, the capital of Judah. Can you guess some of the reasons for the promised destruction? Let's see how well you did by looking up the following references: 1:7, 2:1, 2:2, 2:6, 3:1-3, 3:5-6, and 3:9-11.

In chapter 4, Micah shifts from doom and gloom to hope through the restoration of the gospel. Look for the hope that each of the following would bring.

- 4:1-2 Latter-day temples and the blessings that come from them.
- 4:3-7 The wonder and awe of the millennium.
- 4:10 Zion will be delivered from Babylon.
- 4:11-13 The gathering of the righteous and the wicked through missionary work.

Which did you feel more of today as you studied: hope or doom and gloom?

Day 352, Micah 5-7

Yesterday we finished Micah's prophecies of doom and gloom and began to study the hope of the restoration in the last days. Today, we will study an awesome prophecy about Christ in Micah 5:1-5, so, get ready to mark it up. This prophecy spans from the Assyrians to Rome to the last days. The pronouns "he" and "his" refer to Christ, except in verse 5, when they mean Assyria, or the world. Good luck with that. It may be helpful to read these verses out loud.

Look for what the Lord's people are compared to in the last days in Micah 5:7-8. Verses 9-15 speak of the vengeance and justice of the Lord in the Second coming.

To finish, here are some excellent verses from Micah to help us when we feel overwhelmed by all that is expected of us because we are doing the Lord's work: 6:6-8, 7:7-9, and 7:18-20.

Which did you feel more today as you studied: hope or doom and gloom?

Day 353, Nahum 1-3

One of the most comforting and terrifying quotes I have ever read comes from Joseph Smith and says, "Our heavenly Father is more liberal in His views, and boundless in His mercies and blessings, than we are ready to believe or receive; and, at the same time, is more terrible to the workers of iniquity, more awful in the executions of His punishments, and more ready to detect every false way, than we are apt to suppose Him to be." (Teachings of the Prophet Joseph Smith, p. 257).

These dual attributes of justice and mercy are powerfully shown in Nahum 1. Roughly 100 years after the preaching of Jonah, Nahum declared the destruction of Nineveh. As you study Nahum 1, you will need to mark in two different colors. Use one color to mark words or phrases that show the justice of God. Then, use the other color to mark words or phrases that show the mercy of God.

Nahum can mean "comfort" or "consoler." What about this message is comforting and consoling?

Nahum 2 describes how Nineveh would be destroyed, and Nahum 3 tells why it was destroyed. Mark the phrase "I am against thee" in Nahum 2:13 and 3:5. The Lord's mercy can be for us, or His justice can be against us. When have you felt that God was for or against you?

Day 354, Habakkuk 1-3

Habakkuk clearly saw the unrighteousness in his own people and the utter wickedness in the Chaldeans, or Babylonians, who were destroying his people. What flaw did the prophet think he had discovered in God, according to Habakkuk 1:1-4 and 12-13? Do you have any challenging questions for God?

In chapter 2:1, Habakkuk fully expected a rebuke from God for the tough questions he asked. God didn't respond with a rebuke, but with two answers. The first, is found in Habakkuk 2:4, where it says, "the just shall live by his faith." It takes faith to be and stay righteous in a world where the wicked are not punished as quickly as we want. The second response is found in the rest of chapter 2, showing that the wicked will be punished with great woe. Habakkuk 2:20 is inscribed on an archway in the Idaho Falls Idaho Temple.

Habakkuk chapter 3 is a prayer of awe at the majesty and glory of God. In Habakkuk 3:17-19, the prophet summed up all he had learned. If nothing went well for him, Habakkuk would still rejoice in God (3:17-18). I love the promise that God will transform our feet into "hinds' feet" so that we can walk upon God's high places (3:19). A hind is a small deer. If you have ever seen the difficult terrain that deer, goats, and sheep can handle with ease, then you know the promise of God to us. What are the high places that God has helped you reach so far? What are some of the high places that God will yet help you reach?

Day 355, Zephaniah 1-3

Zephaniah was a prophet during the time of King Josiah. He had two major messages. The first is the complete and unavoidable destruction that awaits the wicked at the Lord's coming. Read any 10 verses in Zephaniah 1:1-18 and 2:4-3:8 and you will find both the cause and means of destruction. Zephaniah's name means "the Lord hides." Are you giving God any reasons to hide His peace and blessings from you?

The second theme that Zephaniah addressed is that God will hide His people from destruction and provide protection. In Zephaniah 2:1-3, look for what a person must do to "be hid in the day of the Lord's anger." This idea of being hid in Christ also comes up in D&C 86:9 and Colossians 3:2-3. Joseph Smith taught that to be hid in Christ is to have one's calling and election made sure (History of the Church 5:391). Some of the blessings of being hid in Christ are presented in Zephaniah 3:9-20. Are you are currently receiving any of these blessings?

A fascinating reference is Zephaniah 3:9, where it is revealed that after the Second Coming, the effects of the Tower of Babel will be reversed.

Day 356, Haggai 1-2

The prophet Haggai was a contemporary with the prophet Zechariah and Zerubbabel, who led the children of Israel back to Jerusalem from Babylon. When they returned, the people began to construct their own houses, but left the temple in waste. In Haggai 1:5-11, look for what blessings the Lord said the people were missing out on because the temple was incomplete.

Several times in these chapters, the Lord, through Haggai, asked His people to "Consider your ways" (1:5-7, and 2:15-18). Consider your own ways. How is your temple attendance and worship? Is it substantial enough to result in all the blessings that God wants to pour down upon your head, house, and community?

The response to Haggai's words was incredible. Look for the reactions in Haggai 1:12-15.

Some who were familiar with the Temple of Solomon were concerned that the new temple lacked the same luster (Haggai 2:1-3). The Lord assured the people that the temple built during the Millennium would outdo Solomon's, but even humbler and homelier temples bring the peace of the Lord (Haggai 1:4-9). When was the last time you felt this promised peace that the temple provides?

Haggai 2:5 was a stirring verse to those who were asked to build the temple. What does God want you to "be strong" at doing in your life?

Day 357, Zechariah 1-2

The prophet Zechariah was a contemporary of Haggai and helped motivate the Jews in the rebuilding of the temple (Ezra 5-6, and Haggai 1-2). Zechariah's style of writing makes him one of the most difficult to understand. If it wasn't for the relatively short length, more people would complain about him than Isaiah. Though there is sometimes confusion from the symbolism, the main themes are plain. As you read Zechariah 1:1-6, what would you say is the major message that the Lord wanted the prophet to tell the people?

Zechariah received eight visions in a single night. We will cover three of them today. They all deal with the building up of Zion and the temple. The first is found in Zechariah 1:7-17 as messengers from God have returned, having observed the conditions of the earth and found peace (:11). The conditions to rebuild the temple in Jerusalem were perfect (:16). The second vision is of four horns, which represented the power of worldly forces to scatter Israel but were being destroyed by the peaceful building of the temple through craftsmen (1:18-21). How does the temple help us from being scattered today?

In the third vision, a man tried to measure a future Jerusalem and was stopped because Zion wasn't all contained within the walls and glory of the Lord was there (2:1-5). The Lord promised that He would dwell with the people if they fled from Babylon, the symbol of worldliness (2:6-13). What worldly thoughts, desires, or actions do you need to flee so that the Lord can dwell in the midst of your mind, heart, and home?

Day 358, Zechariah 3-5

The "BRANCH" mentioned that would, with intelligence and knowledge, identify and remove the iniquity of the people in one day is Christ (Zechariah 3:8-9). In Zechariah 3:1-7, we see how Joshua, the high priest, was cleansed from his sins by the changing of his garments. This is temple talk. We all know the great feeling of changing from filthy clothes into clean clothes. That feeling is magnified when it comes to becoming clean from sin.

In chapter 4, the candlestick represents Zerubbabel, who led the Jews out of Babylonian captivity to rebuild the temple. In Zechariah 4:6, look for how Zerubbabel is to build and how he is not to build the temple. Why can't the temple be built like any other building?

In Zechariah 5, a great roll, representing the coming judgment, is seen flying through the air to cut off those who are unworthy (:1-4). In Zechariah 5:5-11, a wicked woman in a barrel was taken to Shinar, or Babylon. Wickedness will eventually be cast out and returned to its own place.

Day 359, Zechariah 6-8

In Zechariah 6 we see four chariots that go forth in judgment upon the earth, representing the war, mourning, holiness, and confusion that will exist in the last days. Joshua, the high priest, was crowned, symbolically representing The BRANCH, or Christ, who will one-day reign as both King and Priest over the whole earth.

The Jews who had returned from Babylon wanted to know if they should continue to fast in remembrance of the destruction of Jerusalem now that they had returned (Zechariah 7:3). In response, the Lord taught the people about the true purpose of fasting. Look in Zechariah 7:5-10 for the real purpose behind fasting. Which of those reasons made you want to fast better? In Zechariah 7:11-13, we also learn that real fasting will increase the likelihood that God will hear us and that we will hear him.

The great hope and peace promised in Zechariah 8 are for the day in which the Lord will dwell in the Holy City during the Millennium (8:3). As you read this chapter, look for several phrases to mark that make you anticipate that wonderful day.

Day 360, Zechariah 9-11

In chapter 9, we see some extraordinary verses that were fulfilled during the Savior's mortal life, and will yet be fulfilled again when He begins to reign following the Second Coming. What do verses 9-11 say about how He will conduct Himself as a leader? Why do you think it is important that Jesus chose to ride a donkey?

In Zechariah 10:6-12, we see a wonderful example of how the Lord is personally involved with the gathering of Israel. When have you witnessed Him personally gather back one who was lost?

In Zechariah 11, we see that after great destruction, a shepherd comes forth to care for and feed the slaughtered sheep (:1-7). Eventually this shepherd is rejected and paid thirty pieces of silver, a symbol that is later associated with the betrayal of Christ for the same amount (:12-13).

Day 361, Zechariah 12-14

One of the most common phrases you will read in these chapters is "in that day." You may want to mark that phrase as you come across it. This phrase refers to the Second Coming and the Millennial reign of Jesus Christ. Chapter 12 is about the nations of the earth gathering together to wage war against Jerusalem during a battle in the valley of Megiddon, or Armageddon (:11). This battle will stop when Jesus descends from heaven and places his foot upon the Mount of Olives (12:4). This contact will cause the mountain to cleave in two, creating a valley of escape for endangered Jews (14:5). It is in the midst of this newly formed valley that the Jews will meet a figure who has wounds in His hands and feet (12:10). When the Jews ask about these wounds, they will learn that Jesus was the Messiah (13:6). Jesus will become King and Lord over all the earth (14:9). There will be peace, and everything will be built and function with Holiness to the Lord (14:20-21).

These chapters are brilliant, but read out of order at times. A reference that really helps to put things into order is D&C 45:48-53. What are some of the blessings of knowing that Jesus Christ is your Savior now, rather than waiting for Him to reveal His wounds to you as proof?

Day 362, Malachi 1

The people of the Lord during Malachi's ministry did not believe the Lord loved them (:2). To help Israel understand why he couldn't manifest His love by pouring out blessings upon them, the Lord brought up Jacob and Esau (:2-5). Esau appeared to be hated by the Lord, but it was because of the way he discounted the sacred blessings offered to him that resulted in him not being blessed like Jacob.

In verses 6-14, look for how the children of Israel felt about the sacrifices they were making to the Lord. How did the Lord feel about these offerings? Why do you think the quality of the sacrifice is important?

What would the Lord say about the quality of your sacrifices? How well do you do at making the sacrament a meaningful act of worship?

Day 363, Malachi 2

This chapter is written to the priesthood holders of Malachi's day, but many of the warnings can be carried over to our day, and even applied to all members who are supposed to be examples (:1). These leaders will be cursed "if ye will not lay [the Lords counsel and commandments] to heart" (:2). Not even sacred ordinances, like the sacrament and Passover feasts could benefit them (:3).

In verses 4-7, you will see what the Lord expects of those who are the leaders of His people. When have you had such a leader in your life? What would it take for you to become such a leader or an example?

Several times in verses 10-17, the Lord pointed out how these leaders have dealt treacherously, or deceptively with brothers, wives of the covenant, offerings, and in misjudgment of sins. The result of this "partial" keeping of the law was that they caused others to stumble and had no power themselves (:8-9).

Day 364, Malachi 3

Everything in this chapter is to help us answer the questions in verse 2. Who will, and who won't, be able to stand before the Lord, according to verses 1-7? D&C 13 and 128:24 are great cross references for verse :3.

D&C 64:23 teaches that the faithful paying of tithing, or charitable alms-giving, will help us to be able to stand at the Lord's coming. Verses 8-12 contain additional promises from the Lord to the payers of tithing. Why do you think nations are also blessed when people pay tithing? People often want proof that there is a God. In verse 10, the Lord invites all to prove His existence by receiving His promised blessings for payment of tithing. How has the Lord of hosts proved His blessings to you as you have payed tithing?

The conditions of this world sometimes leave us saying the same things recorded in verses 13-15. God's favorite things in this world that He has created are not diamonds, silver, or gold, but the jewels of celestial children who have chosen to become like their heavenly parents (:16-18).

Day 365, Malachi 4

What is the difference between how the wicked and those who reverence and respect the Lord will experience the Second Coming according to verses 1-3?

In the millennium children will be wonderfully blessed and protected, like calves in the stalls (:2). Are there things that you can do in your home right now to provide more protection, comfort, and love for your children?

The teachings of Moses and the Old Testament helped to prepare people for the coming of Christ. We are instructed to remember these teachings, for they will also help us be ready for the Savior's Second Coming (:4).

Before the Lord's Second Coming, what was promised in verses 5-6 that would happen, and why is it an appropriate way to end the Old Testament? This is one of the first scriptures that the angel Moroni quoted to young Joseph Smith. However, it was quoted a little differently than it reads in Malachi. Look in either JSH 1:38-39 or D&C 2:1-3 to see the significant and meaningful differences. Those who don't use this sacred sealing power are cursing or wasting the earth and the purpose for which it was created (D&C 49:15-17). If you haven't yet, will you continue to have at the center of your desires a striving within you to one day have a spouse and children sealed to you? God's great desire is that His whole family might be sealed and brought home to inherit all that they can.

Day 366

Because the gospel is endless, I invite you to continue in your efforts to have daily study. If you need something to assist you, please consider another of my fine books. Thank you for allowing me to be a part of your sacred time each day.

Bibliography

Beck. Julie B. "Teaching the Doctrine of the Family." *Ensign*, August 2009.

Faust. James E. "Responsibilities of Shepherds." *Ensign*, May 1995.

Holland. Jeffrey R. "The Laborers in the Vineyard." *Ensign*, May 2012.

Holland. Jeffrey R. "Remember Lot's Wife" Brigham Young University Devotional. Jan. 13, 2009. Retrieved from speeches.byu.edu

Madsen. Truman G. *Presidents of the Church*. Salt Lake City, Utah: Deseret Book, 2005.

Maxwell. Neal A. "Deny Yourselves of All Ungodliness." *Ensign*, May 1995

Maxwell. Neal A. *We Will Prove Them Herewith*. Salt Lake City, Utah: Deseret Book, 1982.

Maxwell. Neal A. "The Old Testament: Relevancy within Antiquity" Address to S&I on Aug 16, 1979

McConkie. Bruce R. "All Are Alike unto God." CES Religious Educators Symposium on August 18, 1978.

Muhlestein. Kerry. "Ruth, Redemption, Covenant, and Christ," as sited *The Gospel of Jesus Christ in the Old Testament, 38th Annual Brigham Young University Sidney B. Sperry Symposium*. Salt Lake City, Utah: Deseret Book, 2009.

Nelson. Russell M. "Where Is Wisdom?" *Ensign*, Nov 1992.

Old Testament Student Manual: Genesis–2 Samuel. Church Educational System manual. 1981.

Packer. Boyd K. "How to Survive in Enemy Territory." *New Era*, Apr. 2012

Packer. Boyd K. "Prayer and Promptings." *Ensign* Nov. 2009.

Romney. Marion G. "Temples—The Gates to Heaven" *Ensign*, Mar. 1971.

Scott. Richard G. "Trust in the Lord." *Ensign*, Nov. 1995.

Smith. Joseph. *Lectures on Faith*. Salt Lake City, Utah: Covenant Communications, 2000.

Smith. Joseph. Jr. *Teachings of the Prophet Joseph Smith*. Salt Lake City, Utah: Deseret Book, 1976.

Smith. Joseph Fielding. "Fall--Atonement--Resurrection--Sacrament," in Charge to Religious Educators, p. 124 as quoted in *Doctrines of the Gospel Student Manual Religion 430 and 431*. Salt Lake City, Utah: The Church of Jesus Christ of Latter-day Saints, 2004.

Taylor. John. "Discourse Delivered" *Deseret News*, Jan. 16, 1878.

Made in the USA
Lexington, KY
13 November 2019